Susan Travis LMHC, N.C.C.

Your Own Worst Enemy... NO MORE

CONTENTS

Part II Prison Builder Role

INTRODUCTION

Who I am and why I wrote this book

This is a book born from and nursed by three sources: my twenty-eight years as a psychotherapist in private practice; my thirty years as a career counselor at the Rockland County Guidance Center; and my sixty-seven years as a person who is still a work in progress.

In my professional and personal life, I have heard clients, friends, and family say, while shaking their heads, "I am my own worst enemy." I have said it myself on more than a few occasions. Have you ever uttered these words? Or had this said about you?

I decided it was time to address what lies behind this often-said self-imprisoning phrase. I use the analogy of people as prisoners, prison builders, jailers, and key holders to describe the process of becoming one's own worst enemy and the process of escaping from this imprisonment. I wrote this book because of my strong desire to bring consciousness to the unconscious process of self- imprisonment. I wanted to give the reader the tools (Keys) to freedom, along with clear examples of how to use these tools.

Throughout the history of humanity, there have been many references to *humans as prisoners*. It was recognized early on that this is a rich metaphor. Plato used it in his *Allegory of the Cave* (427 BC); Dante referred to *humans as prisoners* in the *Inferno (14th century)*; and even Einstein used this analogy.

A human being is a part of the whole called by us universe, a part limited in time and space. He experiences himself, his thoughts and feeling as something separated from the rest, a kind of optical delusion of his consciousness. This delusion is a kind of prison for us, restricting us to our personal desires and to affection for a few per-sons nearest to us. Our task must be to free ourselves from this pris-on....[1]*[Albert Einstein]*

Consciousness is a state of mind in which you are aware of your own mental processes, thoughts, feelings and senses. You are alert and aware of yourself and the environment. Our "optical delu-sion of consciousness," in Einstein's words, is a consciousness so lim-ited that it's really an imprisoning unconsciousness.

We are all, to some degree, prisoners in our own self-created prisons. In order to change this reality, awareness is essential, along with the desire, willingness and the tools to change. With that in mind, I introduce you to yourself, not only as Prisoner, but also as Prison Builder, Jailer, and Key Holder.

We play all these roles.

This book delves into what it means to play all these roles, how and why you might have begun to play these roles, and, most impor-tantly, how to free yourself from your self-created prisons.

Book Overview

Part I describes three ways you unconsciously make yourself a Prisoner. Negative Self-Talk, Unhealthy Relationship Choices, and Goals that are Setups transform you into a Prisoner.

Part II describes how you become a Prison Builder, and covers twelve Prisons you might have unconsciously built. If reading about twelve Prisons feels like too much information to ingest, go to the prisons whose names you are drawn to; these might be Prisons you have created.

Part III covers the third unconscious role, that of Jailer. Seven Jailers are described in short resume format, using the vehicle of humor to bring awareness to the role.

At the end of each chapter in Parts I, II, and III will be a few questions for you to answer with a check mark. This is a quick means of reinforcing what you have learned as it pertains to you. It also develops into an outline that shows you:

1) How you became a Prisoner

2) What Prisons you built

3) Which Jailers you are.

Part IV examines the first conscious role, that of Key Holder. Sixteen Keys are described in the following chapters: the Master Keys; the Mind Shift Keys; the Potential Expansion Keys; and the Spirit Keys. This is the part of the book that holds the secret to freedom. The sixteen Keys described here can be used individually or in any combination to open the locks of your self-built Prisons. Again, if you feel it is too much to take in at one reading, go to the Keys you believe can help you, or someone you love, out of an unconsciously created Prison. At the end of each these chapters will also be a few short questions to answer with a check mark.

Part V contains five Prison Break stories. Each story is a how-to model for a triumphant Prison Break. The characters in each story are compiled from several different people. At the end of each story, in summarized outline format, you will clearly see how each person became a Prisoner, what Negative Self-Talk filled his or her brain, which of the five Unhealthy Relationship Choices he or she made, and what Goal-Setting Setup he or she used. You will also see which Prisons the person in each story built, and what Jailers vigilantly kept him or her imprisoned. Finally, you will learn which Keys were used for each person's "great escape." These stories will reinforce the lessons of the book. They give you the opportunity to step back and recognize yourself in the choices made by another person. The stories are meant to give you a pattern of escape and the awareness that your freedom is possible.

Part VI is a script for a guided imagery. It allows you, using your new awareness, to personalize your own Prison Break, to become free, and to be Your Own Worst Enemy…No More!

How To Use This Book

Read this book in the way that works best for your style of absorbing information, and that allows you to optimize your enjoyment. If only the Keys interest you, head right for Part IV. If reading stories is a more enjoyable way to take in new information, then start with Part V. I wrote this book to bring your awareness to the unconscious roles you play that keep you imprisoned in a confined life. With this newfound awareness, you can use any of the sixteen Keys offered in this book—Keys you've always had in your possession—to finally unlock your Prison doors and embrace the genuine life you deserve!

Life After Prison

After breaking out of prison, it is time to reevaluate your life, to keep what works and eliminate what doesn't work. The Chinese have two pictorials for the word crisis. These two pictorials literally mean "dangerous opportunity." Breaking out of your self-imposed Prisons is a dangerous opportunity to redesign your life. With that in mind, read Part VI, where you—the exhausted and exhilarated Prison Breaker—will find a relaxing guided imagery to reinforce the skills and tools you used to break out of your Prisons. The imagery will also assist you in envisioning a life of conscious freedom. I invite you to be Your Own Worst Enemy...No More!

* * *

By the end of this book, you will have a profile of:

1) How you make yourself a Prisoner.

2) What Prisons you have built.

3) Which Jailers you are.

4) Which Keys you need to make your own Prison Break.

Part I

Prisoner Role

CHAPTER ONE

Negative Self-Talk

I'm not enough; I'm never going to be; I should

You teach people how to treat you.

Contemplate this for a moment. Go back, read the sentence slowly, and think about what it means.

Here is a simple example: you always say yes to everything a particular person asks of you. What do you teach that person? You teach that person to always expect you to say yes. If for some reason you need or want to say no, this person feels let down. He has come to expect yes because that is what you have taught him. He may have a negative or even outwardly hostile reaction to not having his expectation met.

Here is another example: you have a roommate and the two of you have agreed upon a division of labor. One of your roommate's jobs is to do her own dishes. Every day, dishes pile up in the sink and by the third day, without fail, you wash all of the dishes, even though most of them were used by your roommate.

Guess what? After two months, or less, you have taught your roommate that you will clean any dishes left in the sink for three days. She, therefore, continues to leave dirty dishes in the sink because you have taught her that she can treat agreements with you in this disrespectful manner.

These two examples might be pretty obvious. Less obvious is how you teach yourself to treat yourself like your own worst enemy. Through the use of Negative Self-Talk, you teach yourself that you're really pretty awful, and deserve the verbal abuse that you continue to subject yourself to. As a result of this continuous Negative Self-Talk, a Prisoner is born. Each time you tell yourself, "I'm not enough," "I'm never going to be," or "I should," you reinforce these beliefs and start to act accordingly. If you truly listened to yourself, you would hear all the painful statements that you say on a daily basis. You don't merely tell yourself that you're not smart enough, you use stinging words: stupid, jerk, idiot, and on and painfully on.

You not only tell yourself that you're not lovable enough, you go so far as to strongly suggest that you are unlovable, pitiful, undesirable, and other critical things you would only say to your worst enemy. Your cruel, cutting words make a deep imprint on your mind, body and soul.

Why? Why do you do this to yourself? Why do you talk to yourself in a way that you would only talk to your worst enemy? The answer is…you are your own worst enemy. The real question is, "How did you become like this?"

I'm Not Enough

The "how" is found in your personal history. Maybe early on, adults' facial expressions silently signaled to you that you weren't enough. As an infant or child, you didn't sleep enough, smile enough, respond enough.

Moving along in time, perhaps the subtle—or not so subtle—comparisons began. "Bobby isn't sitting up as soon as Paula." "Netta isn't walking, toilet training, or talking as soon as Trisha." Perhaps your brother or sister was funnier, smarter, better looking, or easier to get along with. As a young child, you couldn't look at your mother or father and say, "Excuse me, I believe that is an inaccurate assessment of my abilities." And it probably was inaccurate, painfully so.

It would have been wonderful if there had been another adult around to say these affirming words for you. Early childhood is a critical time for the development of self-esteem. It's the time you hear, repeat, and begin to believe the language that is used to describe you.

Time moves on; the comparisons broaden and now include the school environment as well as the home environment. A teacher might tell you, in so many words, that you are "not able to get it," whatever "it" may be. You are told you are not smart enough to understand math, to pronounce words correctly, or to play a sport. You start to absorb the negative things that you've been told. Sometimes the words "you're not enough" weren't said or even implied, but you perceived non-verbal signals in this painful way. A perception not challenged becomes reality, and you now feel and act as if it were one hundred percent true. The ownership and perpetuation of "I'm not enough" begins to turn you into your own worst enemy and into a person who deserves to be imprisoned. You do not notice when you start to become a Prisoner.

I'm Never Going To Be

The Negative Self-Talk statement "I'm never going to be" is a logical conclusion if you believe you're "not enough." Since the belief "I'm not enough" is based upon a false premise, the conclusion "I'm never going to be" is also false. The problem is that you don't know this. Some people may have literally told you, eye to eye, that you would never succeed, never be loved, or never be happy. Other killer statements such as, "you'll never learn that," "you'll never meet your goals," or "you'll never be as good as" become accepted as the truth when said to you by the important people in your life.

Your Self-Talk begins to reflect this accepted belief. You start to interpret things people say or do through this negative filter.

Without your awareness of what's happening, a self-fulfilling prophecy starts to take hold. Believing you're not smart enough, you are afraid to try things because you assume you will inevitably fail. How can someone "not as smart as," "not as organized as," "not as attractive as" succeed? You start to pass up opportunities, potential friends and, eventually, your dreams.

Your Negative Self-Talk keeps you in the self-appointed role of an unsuccessful person, a loser, or someone who's "never going to be." You forget to question these negative proclamations because at some point you no longer hear what you are saying to yourself. You don't know why, but you strongly believe you are not enough and you will never be enough.

You treat yourself as if you deserve to be a Prisoner and you become imprisoned in the confinement of Negative Self-Talk. William Shakespeare wrote, "No prisons are more confining than those we know not we are in."[2]

I Should

Next, let's listen closely to the Negative Self-Talk of "I should." All day long, you tell yourself the things you "should" do. Not everything that you tell yourself you should do is negative, but it's the self-damaging "I should" that we are going to examine. This "I should" joins with its close cousins "I'm not enough," and "I'm never going to be" in turning you into a Prisoner and creating yet another reason you believe you deserve to be imprisoned.

How do you know what you "should" do? Who taught you the "shoulds" of your life? How did a life of "shoulds" turn you into your own worst enemy and make you a Prisoner? When did the tyranny of the "shoulds" begin? It began when you were too young to question or to decide which "shoulds" reflected who you truly were.

In the beginning, there was the frequently heard "you should." The family, the society, the religion, and the world condition into which you were born defined the early "shoulds." As a young child, your survival was dependent upon being observant; you absorbed the signals from the people in your environment like a huge sponge. You learned through verbal and non-verbal cues what you "should" do or be to get rewarded. Many of these early "shoulds" were imperative. You should make sure no truck is coming when you are crossing the street. This is a very valuable should. You should chew your food and not swallow it whole is also one of the better "shoulds."

Many of the early "shoulds," on the other hand, were imperative only because they were important to the important people in your life. These "shoulds" were part of their adopted beliefs and values. They subtly or not so subtly passed these on to you and, one day, you accepted them as truth. That was the day the external "you should" became "I should" in your world of Self-Talk.

On another fateful day, you realized you couldn't live up to these "I shoulds." The reason you couldn't, you decided, was because you weren't good enough. This is a conclusion that you—a child—would make, lacking the brain development needed to analyze other people's motivations for their imposed shoulds. It is easier, and probably safer to believe that the adults are right and you are to blame for not living up to their expectations. This Negative Self-Talk, "I'm not good enough," was constantly reinforced, adding fuel to the worst-enemy cycle.

Early on, people gave you signals, or told you outright how you should or shouldn't *feel*. At one point you began to tell yourself "I should feel this way," or "I shouldn't feel that way."

An example of this could be found in the expectations around the birth of a second child. Most people in your family felt very happy that another child was born. Perhaps you didn't feel happy. There was nothing you would have liked more than for your parents to return the child. You silently decided that something must be wrong with you because you "should" have felt happy. As time moved on, yet another "should" was added: the expectation that you should feel like sharing. Again, you didn't feel like sharing and you knew this was something you "should" want to do. To yourself, you seemed more awful by the minute.

Who among us has made it through childhood without hearing "you should be happy" when you felt unhappy, or "you shouldn't be angry" when you felt like breaking something? Most of these conflicts around the "you shoulds" get resolved along the way. Some stick and become proof to ourselves that we're not okay.

During your school years, the opportunities for negative "I shoulds" were endless. The more "I shoulds" you imposed on yourself that you didn't live up to, the more you reinforced your Negative Self-Talk. "I'm not smart enough," "I'm never going to do well enough" and "I should know that" could have been part of your Negative Self-Talk in every grade. If you had the misfortune of having an especially bright and charming sibling precede you in the same school, you might constantly have been told, "Mike was so good at math," or "Betty's handwriting was much clearer." Those comparisons, even if not meant to harm, did harm.

It wasn't necessary to be compared to a family member. You might have started comparing yourself to kids in your class who could do something better than you could. You began to feel "I'm not enough" and "I'm never going to be enough." You told yourself all the things you "should" be. As a young child, or adolescent for that matter, you didn't have the healthy ego strength to realize it was all right to be skilled in some areas and not as skilled in others. Once the external statements became internalized—"I should be better in math. Mike got an A," "I should have clearer handwriting. Betty's is like calligraphy"—they further reinforced your belief that you weren't capable, and at some point you stopped trying.

Actually, you might have been smarter than Mike and Betty. But maybe you weren't comfortable speaking up in class or asking for clarification when the teacher was unclear. You might have frozen on tests or had trouble taking in information when anxious. To you, none of these possibilities mattered. The negative "I should" didn't look for reasons, nor did it question. It fed the development of becoming a Prisoner.

As you grew up, the "shoulds" continued. One day, the world of school was over, and you entered the unknown world of work. You might have been one of the millions who are not sure what they want to do for a living, yet have to earn one. Somehow you got the notion that everybody else knew what he or she wanted to do, and the negative "I should" reared its ugly head.

"I should have taken a course in school that would have qualified me for X; I should know what job I want to apply for; I should have a plan for the future." The fact that you aren't achieving any of these new "shoulds" only reinforces your "not-okayness."

After several years of being employed, or self-employed, you start to tell yourself, and maybe others, "I should be further along in my career path" or "I should be earning Y by now." Where is that authoritative rulebook that says where you should be and what you should earn by a certain time? Perhaps others are earning more than you are, and still others are further along on their career ladder than you are. That may be the truth, but that truth is only negative if your Self-Talk tells you it is, or if you buy into someone else's belief as to how much you should presently earn and what rung of the ladder you "should" be on.

When you read the Key Holder chapter, you will learn how to use the Non-Judging Self-Observer Key (NJSO). You will become aware that you are where you are because of the choices you have made, and you will understand that they were the only choices you were capable of making at that time in your life.

The Negative Self-Talk, "I'm not enough," "I'm never going to be," and "I should" that turns you into a Prisoner comes on in full force when you enter into an intimate relationship. Often the people you choose, by their hurtful words or actions, give you reason to feel you are not good enough, that you should act, look, or even be another way. It is these Unhealthy Relationship Choices, the subject of our next chapter, that make you a Prisoner. Sometimes you've given yourself a life sentence, unless…you find the Key!

Prisoner Role: Negative Self-Talk

Please put a check mark if you've said:

- **I'm not enough** _____

- **I'm never going to be** _____

- **I should be, do, have** _____

CHAPTER TWO

Unhealthy Relationship Choices

"Why did I get myself into this unhappy relationship?"

Maybe you have found yourself uttering this to a close friend, or thinking it silently to yourself. You may not be questioning a romantic relationship—it could even be a relationship with a co-worker or friend that is causing you strife. Regardless of who the relationship is with, if this question has begun to plague you, then you are ready for this chapter. Here, we are going to look at the why of five Unhealthy Relationship Choices. These are the choices, along with Negative Self-Talk, that contribute to you becoming a Prisoner.

You choose someone who…

1) has the negative personality traits of the parent you want or wanted to fix or change.

2) your wounded child recognizes as a kindred spirit.

3) takes up so much of your time that you can't be present for your own health and development.

4) reinforces your Negative Self-Talk.

5) is very different from you.

Now take a breath. You may want to read the list again. Be courageous! Stay aware and as you read, think about who you choose to have in your life. Is there a pattern to your choices? Does one or more of the five Unhealthy Relationship Choices seem familiar? Rather than taking responsibility for your Unhealthy Relationship Choices, it may seem easier to blame the person in your life who is causing stress or unhappiness. However, that is the exact thinking that has led to your imprisonment. If you think anyone but you have the Keys to your freedom, you will always be a Prisoner. Identifying the reasons for your Unhealthy Relationship Choices gives you the power to change those choices, thereby setting yourself free—free from the negative, self-perpetuating patterns of your life. You are not alone. Everyone struggles with relationships. Discovering the *why* of your actions is the first step to changing them.

Let's look at the Unhealthy Relationship Choices, one by one.

1. You choose someone with the negative personality traits of the parent you want or wanted to fix or change.

The following two vignettes will illustrate the premise that you often choose relationships (work, friends, or romantic) with someone who has the negative personality traits of the parent you wanted to fix.

Wendy

After work, Wendy is going to a fundraising dinner that her boss has organized. She is tired and doesn't like parties, but feels it is important that she go to this one. At the cocktail hour, there are at least two hundred people milling around. She recognizes several people, but doesn't know the majority of the attendees. After saying hello to fellow employees and spending a little time in several different groups, she finds herself drawn to a small group of men and women. Only two are prior acquaintances; the others are unknown.

Wendy spends the rest of the evening with Peter, one of the men in the group. He seems to be slightly inebriated all evening, but her conscious mind affirms that this is not unusual in a situation like this one. When he asks her for a date, she quickly accepts. That night she dreams of moths and lemmings.

After dating Peter for six months, Wendy begins to notice that he always brings alcohol when he comes to her house. She tells herself it's because she doesn't drink and therefore keeps no alcohol in her home. Peter has a few drinks before they go to a friend's house for dinner, and always gets that buzz he had the night they met. Now, she notices it isn't just a slight buzz. Wendy's denial is being challenged by moments of clarity. Peter starts not showing up for dates, calling days later with some elaborate excuse.

On their last date, Peter arrived at Wendy's home too intoxicated to drive safely.

Wendy refused to go out with him that night. He turned around and left. As she closed the door, she heard her own voice cry out, "I can't believe, in a room of two hundred people, I picked an alcoholic!" Finally, the protection of Wendy's denial was starting to erode.

Wendy's father had been an alcoholic, and she had sworn to herself she would never be in a relationship with an alcoholic. Peter was the third man she had dated who drank excessively; the first was her ex-husband, Walter. Why? The answer is that Wendy couldn't fix her dad's alcoholism, so she unconsciously sought someone with the same problem in order to have another chance at fixing him. How many more chances does she need?

* * *

Mike

Now, let's look at Mike and the choices he made. Mike had a verbally abusive father. To please his father, he anxiously went over every chore he was given to be sure he made no mistakes. Mistakes were not tolerated and Mike was screamed at and shamed for the slightest imperfection. Over the years, no matter how hard he tried, Mike couldn't do anything right in his father's eyes. Mike's father died at age fifty-two from a massive heart attack. Their relationship was never fixed.

Mike works for a computer software firm, in a department that consists of only eight people. Bill, the manager, is smart, arrogant and verbally explosive. He treats everyone abusively. Mike and his co-workers are overachievers. They work hard and the department does well. Mike has the same stomach problem and painful head-aches he had as a child, and is frequently absent due to illness. He especially dreads the staff meetings. He has missed several, and when he does attend, he sits silently through them. Bill always picks on someone at staff meetings. At one meeting, Mike summons the courage to stand up to Bill, who is mercilessly berating Betty, the youngest team member. Betty strongly resembles Mike's younger sister. Bill punishes Mike for standing up to him, overloading Mike with parts of the job he finds most distasteful. Ernesto, another member of Mike's work family, quits after complaining for a year about the manager's verbally abusive behavior. Three months later, much to everybody's surprise, Ernesto returns to his former position, leaving a job where the department head is easygoing.

One day, when Bill is away and the group is having lunch together, Mike tells everybody that Ernesto's return is making him think about why he stays in such a tense work situation. He asks the group a personal question, "How many of you had a verbally abusive parent?" After a moment of silence, all six of Mike's co-workers raise their hands. Ernesto blurts out, "I couldn't help myself. I was so drawn to come back." Mike hopes that if he works really hard and does well for the team, Bill will appreciate him and be nicer to him.

* * *

In both examples, Wendy and Mike are unconsciously drawn to someone with the negative personality traits or behaviors of the parent each of them wanted to fix. To break this relational pattern, Wendy and Mike need awareness, and then the ability to act on that awareness. They may continue to be drawn to this relationship challenge, but in time, they can learn that even if they continue to be drawn to these "fixer-uppers," they cannot enter the relationship. If they do enter the relationship, they can quickly extract themselves.

It was not your conscious intention to find someone who replicated the negative traits of one or both parents. Conscious intention was not operating in your choice. A very primitive, unconscious motivation was guiding you. Even though this unhealthy choice doesn't fall under the same heading as a moth drawn to the flame or a lemming drawn to the sea, it was fueled by a powerful unconscious need: the need to get it right. Unable to fix the parent who has the same negative traits as your present-day choice, you are going to fix this person.

A part of you, perhaps an unconscious part, longs for a sense of completion. You couldn't fix the alcoholic, abusive, or emotionally unavailable parent, so now you have a second chance. You hope that this representative person will alter his or her negative traits and finally meet your long-unfulfilled needs. You need to get what you never got: attention, intimacy, love, nurturance, or respect. You are creating the same early-childhood drama, with a substitute actor for the parent you needed to fix.

2. You choose someone your "wounded child" recognizes as a kindred spirit.

This Unhealthy Relationship Choice can happen on an unconscious level. In the following vignette, Bess makes this unconscious choice and enters into an Unhealthy Relationship.

Bess

Bess doesn't know the history of the person she feels drawn to at the Sunday garage sale. She realizes she's having an internal monologue as she finds a way to cross the room to interact with a man who is looking at old trunks: *"He's not my body type. He's too stocky. He looks a little disheveled, but there's something appealing about him. What? He doesn't seem to be able to get the attention of the seller. Ask already! I'm annoyed at him and we haven't even met yet. I can't ask questions either. Who am I to get angry with him?"* Bess's anger dissipates when she's standing near the man, and she almost feels protective of his inability to get someone's attention. She tentatively asks the man how old he thinks the trunk could be. Earl is flustered that such an attractive woman has asked him a question, yet he's surprised how comfortable he feels with her in his "space." Earl usually doesn't like people to stand close to him.

After the garage sale, Bess and Earl walk to town and have lunch. They chitchat, talking about their jobs, and how they wound up living in Miami. They touch on family, but skim the surface, not looking directly at each other during this part of their getting-to-know-you conversation. Bess and Earl don't want lunch to end. Both are thinking that they've never felt so comfortable and safe with someone.

Earl calls Bess the next day, and asks her on a breakfast date that turns into a sixteen-hour marathon. When Bess mentions at breakfast that she noticed Earl had a hard time getting the attention of the seller of the trunk, a floodgate of old feelings opens up in Earl. They take a long walk on the beach and discover that they both had traumatic childhoods.

Bess was verbally abused to the point of feeling she had no right to exist. Both of her parents died and she was "taken care of" by an elderly maternal aunt. Her aunt took out her unresolved jealousy and hatred toward her dead sister on her niece, Bess, who was the spitting image of her beautiful mother. All of her life, Bess has felt ugly, useless, undeserving, ungrateful, and all the other "uns" her aunt could throw at her. Her life remains very small and secluded because she uses invisibility as a shield to protect herself from the rejection she believes she will face.

Earl was physically abused by his uncle Luis, his father's youngest brother. Earl's dad traveled all the time, and his mother was overwhelmed by raising their six children on her own. Earl's Uncle Luis helped out, much to his mother's relief, by watching Earl every Saturday. But Luis was a sick man, and used Earl as a scapegoat for his anger and frustration at not being happy, successful, and popular—all the things his personality made impossible to achieve. He hit Earl, twisted his arm, and pushed him around. Earl never knew when his uncle would harm him; there was no rhyme or reason. He was terrorized, and believed, in his child's mind, that he was always doing something wrong. He tried to tell his mother, but, since there were no broken bones, only bruises she thought any child would get, she denied that anything was wrong. She desperately needed her brother-in-law's help.

After several months of dating, Bess and Earl continue to share their childhood stories, and to take comfort in being heard and understood. After six more months of going over their numerous painful childhood wounds, they realize that they have isolated themselves from everyone else. Isolation is familiar, while trying to expand their world has been difficult for each of them. This developing pattern, of just the two of them, feels much safer.

Bess decides not to take a trip to London with a friend—a trip they'd planned before she met Earl. When she tells him about the trip, Earl looks as if he is losing his best friend. He wants Bess with him, especially when he needs to go anywhere that might be crowded and where people might stand too close to him. Bess is his buffer.

Bess and Toby, her only friend at work, have signed up for a self-help course: How To Be Assertive. Earl, wanting to protect Bess, discourages her from taking the course, saying, "People can be angry if you speak up assertively, and they can say hurtful things if you disagree with them." This only reaffirms Bess's own fears, and she withdraws from the course. Slowly, she withdraws from a healthier and more expansive life. That budding voice of health inside Bess is getting weaker and weaker.

When Bess marries Earl, their silent vow is to protect, over and over and over again, each other's wounded child by constantly reminding each other how unsafe the world is. Four months into her marriage, Bess looks out her kitchen window and wonders why she feels so unhappy.

* * *

Childhood, and its multitude of experiences, can be remembered as anywhere from very good to very traumatic. Many childhoods fall between these two extremes, and are remembered as good, good enough, fair, or bad. It is difficult to survive childhood without *some* wounds. These could be as normal as the "boo boo" on your knee that someone kissed to make better, to the traumatic emotional, physical, and sexual abuse perpetrated upon a child. Most likely, they were something in between. In this second Unhealthy Relationship Choice, you might choose a friend or partner whom your wounded child recognizes as a kindred spirit. You make this choice because you have experienced the more traumatic wounds. Your wounds have been stored deep within your body's memory, waiting to resurface when triggered—in this case—by another wounded child.

Deep wounds need time to heal. Part of the process of healing may be to leave the wound uncovered, exposed. It might be necessary to talk it out with friends or family members. A mental health professional or some form of spiritual guidance can facilitate the healing process. It is necessary to air it out so the healing can continue. Even after it has for the most part healed, the wound is not forgotten. There remains a tender, vulnerable spot.

Remembering that the wound exists is healthy. It is unhealthy when it colors your life and all your relationship choices, and when you let others define you as wounded. Maybe they do this out of love and protection. Maybe it's done to keep your world small, and therefore safer. Somewhere along the line, you accept this definition. You adopt the persona of the wounded child. You wear it in your expression, you weave it into your speech, and you project it in your movements. It becomes detectable, on an unconscious level, by those who have also been wounded. They may not have been wounded in the same way, but their wounds are as deep.

The company of someone who has experienced a similar depth of trauma can be comforting. It is healing to be understood, for someone to *really* know, not just say the words, "I know." A friendship or partnership that contains two wounded children can be healthy. It is healthy when you share other, healthy parts of yourselves—when the wound isn't the only attraction.

The Unhealthy Relationship is created when wounded children find each other, not to share the many aspects of a healthy life, or to aid each other in healing, but to keep the wound open. You feed the pain of the wound to keep it present and alive. Frequent conversations about childhood could continue to refuel your anger and hurt. You become partners in victimhood. Your recognition of a shared painful childhood can be validating, but if it's all you do together, there is no room to put the past behind you. Your wounds will only fester. You allow life and all its choices to continue to emanate from that binding wound.

3. You choose someone who takes up so much of your time...(that, for any number of reasons, you can't be present for your own health and development.)

Maya

Maya had the role of caretaker in her family. She was taught, at an early age, that everybody's needs came before her own. Maya thought that it was normal for a little girl to have many chores and to be responsible for siblings only slightly younger than she was. When Maya was old enough to move out of her family home, she began to create a life based on her own needs, likes, and abilities. Although this has been good for her, at the same time she has a feeling of unease. Let us use Maya's situation to illustrate this third Unhealthy Relationship Choice.

Presently, Maya has a full life. She has a job, several friends, hobbies, and a schedule of exercise that is woven into her week. She has just decided to take a dance class, and get back to writing that children's book she has always wanted to write. Life is full and life is good.

This experience of attending to her needs and wants is new and scary in its unfamiliarity.

Maya's last relationship ended months ago. It wasn't until her life started again that she noticed her life had stopped during the four years of a relationship with a man immersed in a "very important" career that took most of his time and energy. He had asked Maya to take care of everything he needed to have done in his life: his daily chores, his social appointment schedule, his doctor appointments and his travel arrangements. Maya had become his personal assistant, his cheerleader, and his sole caretaker. This "assistance" was in addition to Maya's own job, her daily chores, her social schedule, her doctor appointments and her travel plans. Despite her sacrifices, this man had left because he'd felt Maya didn't have enough time to give him. It took Maya a year to get her *self* back, and then Simon entered her life. This new person, Simon, is someone who needs attention. He seems so different from her ex that she doesn't realize she has chosen the same Unhealthy Relationship. Maya has chosen someone who will rob her of the time she needs for her own health and development.

Simon has a trust fund and doesn't need to be employed. He dabbles in a variety of hobbies but is left with a lot of free time. He has money and time and expects Maya to join him whenever she's not at work. This includes nights, quick weekend getaways, and her allotted vacation time. She stops taking her dance class and stops writing that "silly" little children's book (Simon's word), but Maya's life looks good. She has a partner, one who wants to be with her all of the time. She still has a job, and she gets to travel to exotic places, but Maya feels empty and uncomfortable within herself. At the same time, she is comfortable with this uncomfortableness.

In this new relationship, Maya unconsciously sabotages her own life again, giving up her goals and dreams. She wakes up one day and finds herself a Prisoner. Her life sentence is living someone else's life rather than her own. One night, Maya has a dream. She is on trial. Her defense attorney asks why she has committed this crime against herself. The jury has been told that Maya is a repeat offender, and Maya's attorney needs to evoke sympathy for her by the answer she will give in her own defense. What will her answer be?

Different answers go through Maya's mind. *"Maybe I am afraid I can never meet my own goals. How can I have the nerve to think I can write a children's book? How can I spend so much time on myself, walking every morning and taking a dance class, too? What a selfish luxury. If I do these things, will he leave me?"* Her unconscious mind drifts further away and she says out loud to the jury, "He needs me and wants me with him all the time. He says time together is the only worthwhile time. Aren't I lucky? How could I not commit this crime? I do it for love."

Maya dismisses her dream; she remains a Prisoner in her pattern of her Unhealthy Relationship Choice.

* * *

How do you become a Prisoner in a relationship that swallows all of your time and allows no room for your goals and dreams?

This Unhealthy Relationship Choice has two sides. It is a form of self-sabotage, and a surrender of self.

This unconscious self-sabotage can occur in a romantic relationship, in a platonic relationship, or in a family relationship. On the surface you feel good; you're spending time with someone you care about. Your focus is on the "other." You are supportive, available, and loving. While on the surface you feel good, underneath you often feel empty. You have turned away from yourself; you have slowly and quietly surrendered yourself, and now there is no "you."

This Unhealthy Relationship Choice can be unconsciously self-serving. Being so consumed by the "other," you don't have the time to try things you would enjoy and even be good at. But the good news is that you never have to fail or compete, or experience the pain of not living up to your goals and dreams. You can always hold on to "I might have succeeded." Your Unhealthy Relationship Choice makes you a Prisoner, but the Prison sentence is familiar and not as scary as freedom, which is unfamiliar.

4. You choose someone who reinforces your Negative Self-Talk.

This Unhealthy Relationship might be found in many settings. It might be found in your friendships, in your romantic relationships, and even in the patterns you engage in with your employer or coworkers. Uri's experience at work is a good example of how an employer or co-worker can act as a Reinforcer of Negative Self-Talk.

Uri

In his work environment, Uri has unconsciously replaced his family and their negativity towards him with his new "work family," the present-day Reinforcers of Uri's Negative Self-Talk.

Uri's present-day family is composed of people who give him feedback on his job performance. A recent assessment, by Uri's manager, of the work Uri has completed on an important project, isn't relayed in a constructive manner. His assessment is given in a way that is insulting and berating. It reinforces Uri's ingrained belief that he is definitely "not enough." Uri has worked very hard on this project, and before the manager's assessment, he has taken the risk of telling himself that he's done a decent job. But when he leaves the manager's office, his awareness that he has done a decent job is lost.

The manager's negative reinforcement is familiar, and perversely comforting. Uri buys into this negativity, immediately discounting his own flash of positivity and acting upon the Reinforcer's opinion of his performance. As a result, he doesn't think to ask for constructive criticism, which he could use to improve the project. He is so upset and down on himself that he is unable to take in praise about the project, given by his fellow co-workers. Furthermore, his Negative Self-Talk—reinforced by his manager, the

Reinforcer—keeps Uri from asking for a promotion or other compensation he deserves. The worst-enemy spiral deepens.

Sometimes Uri gets fed up, and in a fleeting moment of self-support, he thinks about leaving this negative environment. But the unknown is too scary. Unfortunately, Uri believes he deserves to be seen in the negative light his Reinforcer shines upon him.

* * *

A Reinforcer is a person who communicates to you—in words, through body language, or tone of voice—that you are not enough, and you will never be enough. A Reinforcer also lets you know what you should do to gain approval by meeting his or her expectations. Your unconscious mind seeks out an Unhealthy Relationship with this Reinforcer. It wants to reap the benefits of the reinforcement.

Employers or co-workers are not the only Reinforcers of your Negative Self-Talk. You might not immediately recognize your romantic partner as a Reinforcer. Actually, this reinforcement of negativity might never be recognized as such, because it is too familiar. On an unconscious level you think it is true. You might wake up one day to find yourself in an unhealthy relationship without realizing that "finding" is the unconscious part of choosing.

Tessa's relationship, the subject of this next vignette, will clearly illustrate the Unhealthy Relationship that is formed when you unconsciously find a Reinforcer of your Negative Self-Talk.

Tessa

In Tessa's relationship with Charlie, who is six years her senior, she feels looked after. That's how she describes it to her best friend,

Pat, two months after meeting Charlie at the Department of Motor Vehicles.

At the beginning of the relationship, all of Charlie's suggestions about how Tessa should change things in her life feel like constructive criticism, suggestions, or advice from someone older and more experienced.

About six months into the relationship, when Tessa and Charlie decide to live together, it begins to feel like what it actually is—plain old criticism. There are too many suggestions and too much advice. Pretty soon, it's clear to both Tessa and Charlie that *she*—not Charlie—has problems. The problems are Tessa's. She isn't tall enough, thin enough, clever enough or attentive enough. Furthermore, she doesn't earn enough or help enough around the house.

Charlie has become her negative Reinforcer, reminding her of all the "not enoughs" she's heard growing up, and eventually begins to tell herself. Since Charlie and Tessa believe she isn't enough in so many ways, it follows that she is just "never going to be enough."

Tessa believed this to be true before she met Charlie; her family had said this on a regular basis. Her new relationship with Charlie reinforces this belief, so why should Tessa bother taking that course she's been thinking about? Why join that book club or get into better shape, or try for the promotion at work? This Negative Self-Talk turns into a self-fulfilling prophecy and perpetuates Tessa's belief. Tessa has become a Prisoner of her own Negative Self-Talk. There is no parole for the Prisoner.

* * *

Let's assume that, just like Tessa, you don't want to be in a relationship with someone who will reinforce your Negative Self-Talk. Let's assume that you want to be in a relationship with someone who accepts and supports who you are, and who reinforces your attempts at Positive Self-Talk. If only consciousness ruled the day! Your unconscious mind, sadly, is often the dominant choice-maker.

After years of being seen in a certain way, it becomes difficult to entertain another viewpoint. In a strange way, the present-day choice of the Reinforcer is your way to give credence to the negative opinion your family members had of you.

It might be hard to understand that there are benefits to Negative Self-Talk, and to choosing relationships that reinforce it. One benefit can be safety; when you are a child, it is safer to believe the opinion of the adults that you depend upon for survival than to believe your own opinion. Another possible benefit can be the comfort of the familiar; you begin to internalize others' limited view of who you are, and you begin to play a role that supports its truth. The role becomes familiar. It is difficult to give up what is familiar in exchange for the great unknown. Another benefit can be justification; not being enough is a built-in excuse for not trying, for failing, and for not taking the necessary risks to discover and follow your dreams.

* * *

The reinforced beliefs, "I'm not enough" and "I'm never going to be," shown in our first two vignettes, lay the groundwork for the birth of their close cousin, "I should." One final vignette will make tangible how the "I should" Negative Self-Talk, when strengthened by a Reinforcer, places you in an Unhealthy Relationship Choice.

Connor

The Negative Self-Talk in Connor's Unhealthy Relationship comes from both his internal "I should" litany and his partner Ziva's "you should" reinforcement.

Over the last six years, Ziva has said that Connor should be more understanding, should be earning six figures, should dress better, should be more organized, should invite her family more often and pay for their airfare, should know what she needs, and on and on and on.

Connor's relationship with Ziva reinforces his own negative "I should." Connor comes from a family of overachievers. Not a day goes by that he isn't reminded of what he should do, feel, want and look like. No one has ever supported who Connor is, but rather who Connor isn't. Connor, from the start, strives to fit Ziva's "you shoulds." He fails miserably. She only wants what's best for him, he tells himself—the same thing he told himself about his family, as his way to survive. Ziva gets away with these hurtful verbalizations because of Connor's underlying belief in their truth. He is a prisoner of her impossible "you shoulds." Every "should" she utters is another bar of his Prison.

* * *

Uri, Tessa, and Connor all picked a Reinforcer, and a Reinforcer also picked them. This Reinforcer might have unconsciously been in wait for someone who felt "not enough," or "less than" so that he or she could feel "more than." Any relationship is a dance in which both partners do familiar steps. In an unhealthy relationship, based on the reinforcement of one partner's Negative Self-Talk, the partners keep stepping on each other's toes and causing constant pain.

When you are your own worst enemy, you will often pick a potential enemy for a partner, one who reinforces your Negative Self-Talk instead of helping you reexamine this negative view.

5. You choose someone who is *so* different from you.

Devon's relationship with Fiona is a good example of the Unhealthy Relationship formed when you choose someone who is *so* different from you. Devon is unconsciously drawn to his polar opposite. Her magnetism is blinding!

Devon

Devon is a quiet man. He has worked with his Uncle Max for the past twenty-two years as a fine cabinetmaker. Devon has become a partner in the small company, and now his uncle is starting to ease out, heading toward retirement. Devon lives in a twelve-hundred-square-foot home on a lake, in a wooded area of the town where he was born. He is forty years old and has never been married, although he has had two long-term relationships. He has a close-knit family—four siblings and nine nieces and nephews.

Devon lives within his means. He takes care of himself, and keeps himself in good condition by hiking in the Shawangunk Mountains near his home. He is the oldest child, and still feels a responsibility for his grown sister and brothers, something he took on after the sudden death of his mother, when he was fifteen. He is also exceptionally handsome, which he doesn't notice, but which is often noticed by the women he meets.

Lately, especially after the recent death of his father, he has been feeling lonely. His four-year relationship with Trisha ended six years before, and his relationships since then have lasted only six months or less. Trisha and Devon were very much alike. Trisha got along well with his family. Why couldn't he commit when she wanted to marry him? He is just starting to ask himself this question. Because of his loneliness, Devon agrees to go with his friend, Eric, to a party in Manhattan that a mutual friend is throwing for his wife's fortieth birthday. Devon rarely goes to the city. The noise, the crowds, and the air quality are so opposite from the environment Devon is comfortable in. Devon normally refuses any party invitation.

When Fiona walks in the door, Devon actually feels himself being "pulled" in her direction. She is pulsing energy from her five-foot-eight-inch frame. Her clothes are floating around her, Devon thinks, and her laugh is infectious as she greets Eric, who is heading toward her. Devon talks to her briefly and, although she wanders off to talk with other guests, Devon stays infused with her energy. She is nothing like Trisha or his first love, Yvonne. Though he is sure Fiona has forgotten him the minute she leaves their conversation, Devon's thoughts of her linger all week. He's never met anyone like her before, but now that he has, his loneliness intensifies.

Surprisingly, Eric calls at the end of the week to say that Fiona has asked a lot of questions about Devon and hinted that she would like him to call her. Devon makes that first call and the next year is a whirlwind. Fiona and Devon have an intense physical chemistry that makes up for their incompatibility in other areas. At first, Devon is flattered that Fiona wants him to spend all of their alone time at her place in the city. "Your house is a bit small," she says, with her alluring smile. He misses his alone time in his home but wants to be with her. He goes to more parties in one year than he has in his entire life. He can't wait to leave them, but he still enjoys watching Fiona flow around the room. Devon and Fiona value fitness and work out together, which is a positive way to spend time together. Fiona says she likes Devon's family; Devon's family doesn't like her. They have reservations because of her flamboyant appearance and her lifestyle that is so different from Devon's preferred lifestyle.

One of Devon's and Fiona's big differences starts to undermine their initial magnetic pull: their very different attitudes toward handling money. Both Devon and Fiona do well financially. Devon is not a spender, but Fiona is. Devon, though he has no children, looks ahead and is saving for college educations he might one day need to pay for. He wants to help his nieces and nephews. Fiona has no children and lives in the moment. "Why save for something that might never happen?" Fiona asks. "Why deprive myself of the life my hard-earned money affords me?"

Devon realizes his spending has doubled in the time Fiona has been in his life. He reluctantly agrees to go on a very expensive vacation, traveling first class, staying at five-star hotels and going on expensive tours and to even more expensive nightclubs. At each juncture, they argue. Fiona wins each time, but Devon withdraws more and more and gets angrier and angrier with himself, for not saying no to what he considers excess.

Their differences are, for the most part, balanced by an intense sexual chemistry, but even this is affected by Devon's discomfort with the extravagant gifts Fiona lavishes on his nieces and nephews.

At the end of their first year as a couple, Fiona feels they should buy a house together. Devon's place is so small, she begins to say—without her alluring smile. It is time to live together, she insists, over and over again. Devon is still drawn to Fiona's energy, an energy he doesn't have and that he admires. He is also drawn to their sexual intimacy. This intimacy is much less frightening to Devon than other forms of intimacy he experienced with Yvonne and Trisha. Even the strong pull he feels toward Fiona isn't enough for him to give up his home, but he agrees to share a rental with her for one year. Fiona picks more expensive apartments to look at than Devon would consider, although with their combined incomes, they can afford this high price range. Fiona shows Devon apartments in busy midtown Manhattan, close to the theater district, where she is presently working. In a fearful moment, when Fiona hints that the relationship will be over unless Devon agrees to this eighteen-hundred-square-foot apartment in the heart of the city, he acquiesces.

Devon sits in their beautifully decorated apartment, in the very noisy heart of the big city, far from lakes and woods. He has to commute back and forth to his business in Pine Bush every day. As each day passes, the feeling that he is a prisoner grows. In fact, Devon *is* a prisoner, a Prisoner of the Unhealthy Relationship that is formed when you choose someone *so* different from you.

* * *

We have all heard the saying, "Opposites attract." The saying we never hear is, "Opposites attract, at first, but without enough common ground, an Unhealthy Relationship can form." This second saying is too long to be catchy, but it is worth investigating before entering such a diametrically opposed union.

Attraction can be strong. Think of the forceful magnetic pull of positive and negative poles in magnets. When you enter the magnetic field of someone so unlike yourself, it is similar to this intense magnetic pull. Does that instant loud "click" deafen you to the signals outside the force field that is created by this type of connection?

A person so different from you could pique your interest. His or her differences could bring newness to your life. When you meet someone like this, you are introduced to new points of view; maybe you have new experiences, are exposed to different cultural or religious beliefs. It might be as simple as an introduction to new foods, movie genres, sporting events, or travel destinations. Everything feels new, different and exciting. You are magnetized. You might have a sense that this person, in some way, completes you, adds to the pieces you've been missing. Maybe you have been too structured, and this person has a "go with the flow" philosophy. This person believes you should live for today, that you should spend now because tomorrow may never come. If you are a loner and like to read on rainy days, take walks alone, or spend hours in your studio doing your favorite hobby, this new partner is your opposite. This partner is always social, gets you out of the house, introduces you to people in his or her circle, perhaps brings you to watch sporting events with groups of friends who have indoor tailgate parties before the game.

The relationship with someone who is different from you can be positive and can add dimensions to your life, but when someone is *so* different from who you are and what you value, then your very being is constantly challenged. If your partner's perspective, lifestyle, energy level and values are polar opposite from yours, then you know this person is not just different from you, but *so* different that you become a Prisoner of an Unhealthy Relationship Choice.

You make yourself a Prisoner when you enter, and remain in, an Unhealthy Relationship. The relationship now becomes the Prison. Unhealthy Relationships are often a continuation of early relational patterns. These patterns, and your role in them, developed before you had the ability or opportunity to create a different experience. You played your role as a way to survive. You played it safe. The patterns, and your role in them, became familiar, and you unconsciously continue to seek out the familiar. Until you become conscious, and change what is unhealthy in that relational pattern, you will remain a Prisoner of Unhealthy Relationship Choices.

Prisoner Role: Unhealthy Relationship Choices

Put a check mark next to the Unhealthy Relationship(s) you have chosen:

1) Someone who has the negative traits of the parent you want or wanted to fix or change. _____

2) Someone your wounded child recognizes as a kindred spirit._____

3) Someone who takes up so much of your time that you can't be present for your own health and development._____

4) Someone who reinforces your negative self-talk. _____

5) Someone who is *so* different from you. _____

CHAPTER THREE

Goal Setting: The Setup

Goals come in all shapes and sizes. They run the gamut from how to change your bad eating habits to how to change your life's direction. Setting doable goals can move you forward toward who you want to be and what you want to achieve. Doable goals are made up of small, manageable steps. They have a reasonable timetable for each of those steps. If you seem unable to move forward, a reevaluation of the goal is made. These doable goals will not make you a prisoner. The five Goals examined in this chapter, on the other hand, are Setups for failure and will imprison you. Why would you set yourself up for failure? Because you set these goals from an unconscious state, and don't realize that they are impossible to attain. In reading the stories of people who have used these five Goal-Setting practices, notice if there is a familiar ring to any of them.

Five Goal-Setting practices that are Setups.

1) **You don't set a goal.**

2) **You try to meet a goal that someone else set for you.**

3) **You set a goal with unrealistic expectations for who you are at the time you set it.**

4) **You set goals and don't focus on the process. You only focus on the outcome. You give yourself no credit for embarking on the journey.**

5) **You don't examine your nature and personal rhythm. Are you genuinely more of a "be"-er or more of a doer? Is**

your rhythm more like a Sunday morning, or more like a full-throttle Monday?

Your unconscious creation of these Setups and your participation in the Setup patterns that develop contribute to your role as a Prisoner.

1. You don't set a goal.

Let's look in on the life of Albert. His story illustrates what can happen when you don't set goals.

Albert

Albert is a smart man on paper. He has a high IQ, is a good test taker, and had a 3.9 Grade Point Average in college. All who know Albert well call him "Mr. I'm not sure." This is a painful label, even when it's said in good fun, because it's true. Albert has always struggled with decisions. He is unable to trust his own desires. His authoritative and arrogant father constantly challenged Albert's desires. His father was a daily list-maker and a goal-setter.

By the time Albert entered middle school, he no longer knew what he wanted, or even what he liked. He didn't trust himself. He was teased and, at times, bullied. The other children sensed his Achilles heel—his chronic uncertainty. An aura of wishy-washiness enveloped him. The kids took advantage of his weakness. This only reinforced Albert's anxiety about making decisions. By the time he was five years old, his inability to set goals had become ingrained.

If Albert was forced to choose something—an article of clothing, an activity, or an instrument—he would only decide at the final hour, when the pain of not choosing became too great. But Albert was not happy with the article of clothing, the activity, or the instrument he forced himself to choose. Because of this, his outcomes were not successful. He was berated for his failures and his lack of well-thought-out goals. As a defense against the hurt of these repeated failures, he decided not to set any goals, and to just let things happen. His mantra became "I can't fail if I never set a goal."

When Albert's father was fed up with him, he left Albert to his own devices, and instead focused his energy on his two list-making, goal-setting children. When Albert was in his third year of high school, while others were looking at colleges, or deciding what job they could find right out of school, Albert was busy avoiding these life path decisions. He only applied to the local community college because his mother suggested it. Albert was easily accepted. At the end of two years, he graduated magna cum laude, but he hadn't set any goals for the next step he would take. He told himself, "I'll see what happens," his protective credo.

Albert wound up doing his last two years at a school his friend Liam had applied to; Albert was getting the same degree in art history that Liam had chosen. A few weeks before graduation, Liam told Albert that he planned to go to graduate school for museum management and art acquisition. Albert's girlfriend of three years wanted to get married and was pushing Albert for a commitment.

On Albert's graduation day, he began to feel anxious. He started to sweat and feel dizzy during the ceremony.

He realized that he had no idea what he wanted to do next. He had set no goals for himself, but had floated freely through these two years of college. "At least," he reminded himself, "I've had no disappointments, no rejections, no failures. So why do I feel unhappy and afraid?"

Why did Albert feel as if he was in a box, dizzy, sweating, and unable to take a step in any direction? His goal-setting motto, "set no goal," had made him a Prisoner. Albert's self-imprisonment didn't happen consciously. His non-goal-setting practice was an unconscious reaction to a father who constantly challenged his decisions, and who demanded that Albert be a list maker and fervent goal setter, traits that were natural to his siblings but not to him. In seeking to avoid the pain of a wrong decision and his father's anger, Albert had created the greater pain of the chaos caused by not setting a goal.

* * *

Why, like Albert, wouldn't you set a goal? It can be an unhealthy reaction to the painful failure of not meeting previous goals you have set. If, after you fail to meet a goal, you step back and examine what the problems are, and change what needs changing about the goal itself, or about you in relation to that goal, you engage in a healthy goal-setting process. This is a process that moves you forward on your chosen path. Engagement in this process doesn't allow you to become a Prisoner.

You make yourself a Prisoner when you don't step back and reevaluate; when you suffer the deep pain of an erroneous assumption that you will always fail. To avoid this deep pain, you no longer set goals. This self-taught, non-goal-setting behavior sets you up for a Prisoner's life. You unconsciously say to yourself, "It's hard to fail at meeting my goal if I never set one." This seems like a fail-safe method of avoiding the pain of failure, but it can have an even more painful result.

Early in life, you might have been given the message, verbally or by the way you were treated, that you weren't good enough. You took in this negative message and reinforced it with your own Negative Self-Talk ("I'm not good enough," "I'll never be..."). When this became your self-perception, it was too frightening to trust that you could meet a goal you had set. You couldn't visualize yourself as successful. You didn't believe you were capable of doing what was needed for a successful outcome. You didn't feel that you deserved a successful life.

The attainment of a goal is the end product of good planning. Goal setting is a vehicle of forward movement. If your fear of using this vehicle is too great, you won't be able to avail yourself of its benefits: the benefits of getting what you set out to obtain and of the self-esteem that comes from that attainment. If you avoid setting any goals, you find yourself in a haphazard universe. Its looseness has a certain freedom. Often this freedom allows you to go around and around in circles, but each time, you wind up where you started.

2. You try to meet a goal that someone else set for you.

The stage is set at an early age for Setup No. 2. Let's look at Hannah's story.

Hannah

Hannah was named after her beloved maternal grandmother. According to everyone, she was the spitting image of her grandmother. "Our little Hannah" was the constant refrain.

Hannah's grandmother was a very artistic woman. Her creativity showed up in the ambiance of her home, in her appearance, and in her artistic endeavors. By making hand-woven shawls, she made a healthy contribution to the support of her household while Hannah's mother was growing up. Hannah remembered the sight of the warp and woof, and the sound of the large wooden loom in her grandmother's studio. She loved the shelves filled with colored wool that covered every wall. When Hannah was ten, her grandmother died suddenly, of a heart attack.

In truth, Hannah's similarity to her grandmother stopped at their appearance. Her mother and her aunt insisted that the similarity went beyond appearance. This similarity myth was perpetuated by their need to keep their mother alive through Hannah. Hannah grew up torn between her mother's and aunt's need for her to be an artistic woman with a love of weaving, and her own blossoming love of science and math. For their sakes, for their attention, for their love, she tried and tried to be artistic. Each unsuccessful try made her feel bad, and then inadequate. Her Negative Self-Talk reaffirmed that she wasn't enough, and was never going to be. It also reminded her that she "should" continue to improve her weaving skills, that she "should" love to do what her grandmother loved, and that she "should" want to be artistic. She did not.

Hannah liked order, numbers, and facts. To her, mathematical solutions were the warp and woof of happiness. However, in the spirit of the Goal-Setting Setup No. 2, she took art classes every summer and applied to the Pratt Institute, a well-respected art school in New York.

Hannah's acceptance letter from Pratt arrived, to the overwhelming joy of her mother and her aunt. As she was getting ready for her first day of classes, Hannah slowly put on her Prison garb and began her four-year sentence.

* * *

People who choose Setup No. 1 find themselves prisoners of Setup No. 2 as well. If you don't set a goal for yourself, you might take what looks like the easy path and let others set goals for you.

This type of goal setting is an effective way to ensure your role as a Prisoner. With the support of the Negative Self-Talk that will inevitably follow, the longevity of your Prisoner status is assured. It can be hard to meet a goal you set for yourself, yet even harder to meet one set by someone else.

Why would anyone set a goal for you? Who would do this? Goal setting by others can pre-date your birth. Goals may have been set for you by well-intentioned family members like Hannah's, by friends, and even by the society into which you were born. The goal setting by others can range from unconscious wishes to fiercely driven plans. Beware, little person!

Some early pre-set goals may sound like this: "We're leaving for the hospital; our little baseball legend is about to be born."

"He's only eleven months old and he said "dog." He's smart like his grandpa; that boy's a chip off the old block. He'll go far!" "I started at four; Mia's six already. I loved ballet class, and so did my mom. But Mia cried again today."

"Our family goes to *this* school. What do you mean you don't fit in? Try harder!"

"She climbed a tree again. Last week we got a call that she was skateboarding with the boys in the bank drive-through. What should we do?"

These friends and family members are not necessarily "evil others," but they have their own dreams, hopes, agendas, and sometimes vicarious wishes that they subtly, or not so subtly, let you know as you grow up. Of course you want to please them. In some cases, it's not safe to go against them. You haven't had the chance to get to know what you are naturally good at, what you like, or who you are.

You first come to earth with a unique set of physical, mental, and emotional attributes that make up who *you* are. Your body rhythm, your innate skills, and even your interests are already encoded in your DNA. On a deep level, these are known to you, or at least, sensed by you. In the quiet moments throughout your life, they may even be "remembered" by you.

3. You set a goal with unrealistic expectations for who you are at the time you set it.

Our next story follows Orlando, who is a prisoner of Setup No. 3.

Orlando

Orlando is from a close-knit, extended family. He is the eldest son in a family of four sons and three daughters. His father's elderly parents recently came to live with Orlando's family and both his father and mother work very hard to support this eleven-person household.

Everybody in his family does his or her part at home, but Orlando, the eldest son, is expected to carry a heavier load. Orlando expects the same of himself. Once, he overheard his father asking his mother if she could take a short leave of absence from her job until they could get some help with his parents, or find an appropriate and affordable facility to put them in. Upon hearing this, Orlando set a goal to do even more to be of help.

Orlando is a junior in high school. He needs a full scholarship to be able to go to college. He's starting to explore different colleges to see which would offer him a scholarship to play varsity soccer. Orlando is the best goalie in his region. He knows scouts will be watching him this year. He was lucky to find a part-time job that accommodates both his academic and soccer schedules. Now, after overhearing his parent's conversation, he's decided to set a goal to find a second part time job so he can help out even more. He feels very nervous about doing this because he knows he has to do exceptionally well on the soccer field this year to ensure his full scholarship. Orlando can usually discuss his problems and worries with his parents, but feels he can't because they are so stressed by their present situation. He wouldn't want them to feel guilty that he is considering a second job.

After several sleepless nights, Orlando decides to apply for a job to take care of a ninety-three-year-old man for two hours after the man's caretaker goes home at 7:00 p.m. The job entails helping him wash up, making sure he takes his medicines, and making sure he is safely in bed by 9:00 p.m. The man's family knows Orlando's family, and knows he is responsible. This Setup adds Orlando to its Prison population.

After two months of going to school, going to his practices and games, working two part-time jobs, doing his homework and his home chores, Orlando, all of sixteen, is starting to wear down. In his run-down state, he is catching every cold he's exposed to. His body can't relax and his sleep is affected. He is starting to get panic attacks, something unfamiliar to his family, and they are very frightened for him. The last straw is an important soccer game that is lost because Orlando is inattentive and does not protect the goal. When his coach approaches him, he breaks down.

The coach calls Orlando's family. Orlando finally tells them how worried he is about the family's finances, how worried he is that they are so stressed, and that his grandparents are getting old. Orlando is used to meeting goals he sets and he is ashamed that he can't carry the load he has put on himself.

Orlando is a very capable young man, a very responsible young man, yet Orlando couldn't successfully accomplish his goal of working a second job, at the time in his life that he set that goal. What he did accomplish was to set himself up to become a Prisoner.

A very fine line, a line that is hard to see and to assess, governs this Setup. Many people cross the line and unknowingly become

Prisoners in the process. People who make themselves prisoners through this third Setup can often be heard saying, "I'm so overwhelmed," or "Maybe I could sleep less,," or "I'm a bundle of nerves," or "I should be able to do this. What's wrong with me?"

What's wrong with you? What's wrong is that you've set an unrealistic goal and you can't face that fact. Why is it unrealistic? Because the person you are at the time you set it is unable to meet that particular goal.

4. You set goals and don't focus on the process. You only focus on the outcome. You give yourself no credit for embarking on the journey.

Suki, the subject of this short story, fell into the trap of Setup No. 4.

Suki

Deciding to start an exercise program, Suki set a goal to walk one and a half miles a day. Suki had been ill much of the winter and early spring. At the time she set this goal, Suki was out of shape. She hadn't exercised in seven months, and it was August, the hottest part of summer.

The first day, Suki managed a half-mile with great difficulty. She forgot to bring water, and she started at the pace she used to walk, but couldn't sustain now. That night, her Negative Self-Talk ran wild. The "not good enough" and the "I should" bounced off the walls. Suki never recognized that the half-mile she'd walked was farther than she had walked since her recovery from illness.

Suki's mistake could also come under the Setup that felled Orlando (Setup No. 3: You set a goal with unrealistic expectations for who you are at the time you set it.)

Determined to meet the mile-and-a-half goal the next day, Suki got up at 6:00 a.m. to beat the heat, carried a water bottle and went a tad slower than her pre-illness pace. Suki made three quarters of a mile with the aid of these modifications. A healthy goal setter would have felt good that there was improvement. The process was in place and working. But Suki, being a Prisoner to Setup No. 4, was mortified that she had made these changes and still had not succeeded. Success for Suki was only accomplished if she completed one and a half miles.

This second "failure" put her into a mild depression. Her Negative Self-Talk was upped a notch and she told herself that her walking days were over, that she was disabled, and that she couldn't bear to try again the next day because it was too devastating that she couldn't meet such an easy goal.

Despite the praise of her family, friends, and doctor for being able to do three quarters of a mile under such conditions, Suki abandoned her goal. Suki set herself up to remain a Prisoner and kept herself from taking credit for embarking on the journey.

* * *

Setup No. 4 is a tough taskmaster. It deems completion the only thing worthy of success. It is uncompromising, single-focused, and inflexible. The self-created Prison system is its greatest fan because this Setup produces enough Prisoners to fill a multitude of Prisons. If you don't reach a goal, and you believe that neither trying nor learning something on the journey to that goal are of value, the Prisons of Self-Judgment, Rigidity, and Shame (which you will read about in the next chapters) take you Prisoner.

When you choose Setup No. 4, you're not interested in the process or the journey of healthy Goal Setting. Your *only* interest is a successful outcome. There's no tolerance for trying to reach a goal, which is a natural element when attempting something you have not done before, or something you have done but find difficult to sustain or repeat.

This Setup shuns and disrespects the only questions worth asking when you set a goal: Where was I? Where am I now? Where do I want to be?

5. You don't examine your nature and personal rhythm. Are you genuinely more of a doer or more of a "be"-er?

Fran

Fran was born with a "bbb-aa-bbb" rhythm. What, you might ask, is that? Begin to clap slowly, with a leisurely pace. After a while, speed up your clapping, but only for a short time; then return to the slower, more leisurely clapping. This is Fran's natural rhythm. Of course, Fran doesn't consciously know her rhythm is "bbb-aa-bbb." Even if she did know, she'd try to ignore it, because her family (nuclear and extended) has a very different rhythm: "aaaa-b-aaaa."

At an early age, Fran was drawn to sitting at her bedroom window and watching the sun peek out between the New York City skyscrapers. She'd listen to the sounds of the city waking up: the whoosh, whoosh of the street-cleaning trucks; the clanking of the store gates being pulled up on the avenue; the occasional horn beeping and ambulance siren whirling during the early-morning activities. Fran also heard the active feet of her family as they got ready for the day ahead; she heard her name constantly being called to "hurry up," to "stop daydreaming," and to "get a move on." Fran was an innate "be"-er in a doer environment. Setup No. 5 awaits its unwitting prisoner.

Fran's mother ran their household like a finely tuned clock. Fran's mother was the taskmaster behind Fran's hunt for her first job as a paralegal. Fran knew she didn't want, nor was she able, to be a corporate lawyer like her mother. If Fran had understood about rhythm, she'd have realized that her rhythm was totally out of sync with the rhythm of a corporate law environment. She would have realized that this was an important factor in her inability to hold that fast-paced job.

Fran's mother agreed to let her take a paralegal course, if she promised to revisit the idea of going to law school in two years. Fran was hired by a high-powered law firm with the help of her mother's large professional network. After three weeks on the job, she started to have severe stomach pains. Fran was smart and was able to do the work, but she struggled to keep up with the pace, a pace that was not her own. All the other employees seemed to thrive in the fast-paced atmosphere. If Fran had had the courage to disappoint her mother, she would have acted upon what she recognized her first day on the job, that "one of these things doesn't belong here." Fran ignored her own rhythm, but not without great consequence. She set herself up to become a Prisoner.

* * *

"Who am I?" This is a question you might ask yourself at different points in your life. Actually, it's a very healthy question, because that "I" is ever-changing. However, some questions that would help you identify your "I" might never be asked. Either you don't know what question to ask, or you are too afraid of the answer to risk asking the question. By nature, you have your own time clock, your circadian rhythm. If left to its own devices, your body will let you know the amount of sleep it requires, the pace at which it best functions, and an overall rhythm that it "dances" to for optimal health and well-being. Your natural pace could be slow and gentle, moderate, or fast and frenetic. Is your rhythm more like a Sunday morning, or more like a full-throttle Monday? Either is fine, if genuine to your nature.

If you are a Prisoner of this Setup, you don't ask these questions of yourself. Even if you discover your natural rhythm and pace, you don't honor the discovery. You end up paying the consequences of this self-denial by becoming a Prisoner, locked into a world spinning too fast or too slowly for your comfort. At some point, you forget that you are living at a pace that is contrary to your rhythm—a pace that is painfully unnatural.

Not honoring your natural rhythm is the unhealthy Setup. Healthy people find a balance between doing and being, but Setup No. 5 occurs when you are out of balance and the pendulum has swung in a direction opposite to your innate nature. You sense that something is out of whack, but you are afraid to ask yourself questions because you're not yet ready to make the changes the answers might suggest.

Societies, cities, industries, families, and relationships have their own pace. Sometimes, in order to fit into the geographical rhythm, your nuclear family's pace, and the pulse of your school, work, and relational environments, you unconsciously go against your natural rhythm.

Maybe you are a "be"-er and your environments might demand that you be a doer. The message you get might be, "We are hard workers, and our family doesn't just sit around," or "Produce, produce, produce!" This might be the hue and cry at your workplace. There is value in hard work, in being active, and in producing. It's necessary to keep a country, family, workplace, and relationship viable. So you do and do and do. You always seem to be trying to catch your breath. As you put the last check on your twenty-four-item "to do" list, you have a gut feeling that something is wrong. But what? A little voice inside your head says, "Perhaps the goal of doing twenty-four things today is too much for your rhythm and nature. Five things would work for you." On the other hand, you may be a doer but be born and raised in a "be"-er family environment. They aren't in a rat race. Actually, they're in no race at all. Your family has a "go-with-the-flow" philosophy and pace. You pick a partner of the same mind because it's so familiar. You often find yourself feeling antsy and champing at the bit. Your Self-Talk goes something like this: "Let's go! Let's go, already! I can't believe you want to "veg" out again this weekend. Soon you'll turn into a vegetable!" Of course, you don't say this out loud. You can't say it out loud because you can't afford to let yourself become aware of your continual discomfort, your lack of ease in this role.

You are a doer in a sea of "be"-ers.

You try to set a goal to "chill" with your family on the weekend. What you don't let yourself know and honor, since it makes you so different from the rest of your family, is that chilling for you is doing things, accomplishing tasks, and meeting multi-level goals. Your family's chilling is very stressful for you.

When you aren't conscious of your own nature and rhythm, you lose touch with yourself. It is therefore hard to make decisions and set goals that show awareness and respect for who you are. Not only do you create Setup No. 5, but because you don't know who you are and what you want, you might also set yourself up by not setting a goal (Setup No. 1). Or you might let others set goals for you (Setup No. 2), or even set a goal with unrealistic expectations for who you are when you set it (Setup No. 3). See if you can clap out your personal rhythm.

* * *

These five Goal-Setting Setups, along with Negative Self-Talk and Unhealthy Relationship Choices, can turn you into a Prisoner. A Prisoner is an unconscious role you play; one that has become ingrained from years of practice. The next unconscious part you play is a supporting role to the Prisoner. It is the role of the Prison Builder. Every Prisoner needs a Prison to keep him or her confined.

In the next chapters, we will explore twelve Prisons that the Prisoner has constructed, using age-old materials as the foundation of each Prison.

Prisoner Role: Goal Setting (The Setup)

Put a check mark next to the Goal-Setting Setup(s) you have set:

1) You don't set a goal. _____

2) You try to meet a goal someone else set for you. _____

3) You set a goal with unrealistic expectations for who you are at the time you set it. _____

4) You set goals and don't focus on the process. You only focus on the outcome. _____

5) You give yourself no credit for embarking on the journey. _____

6) You don't examine your nature and personal rhythm. Are you genuinely more of a "be-er or more of a doer?_____

Part II

Prison Builder Role

CHAPTER FOUR

Prison Builder

You enter earth. Perhaps you are entering with some ready-made genetic propensities and some personality traits carried from the womb. You might even come in with unfinished business from a previous life if that's what you believe.

Yet you still have an opportunity for wonder, and an opportunity to sense your own divinity, an opportunity for joy and to have an open heart. You're still in touch with who you are and your connection to all other beings. Breathe in the memory of these precious moments, because now it begins. The expectations, the hopes and dreams of your family circle are around and immediately put upon you: "We have to keep an eye on this one, she looks just like Aunt Harriet." "He has the long fingers of a pianist; we have another family musician." Your life goals are set for you before you leave the nursery. Sometimes you are born to a family that is not ready to have a child. You are too young to understand that the problems this lack of readiness causes lie within the family member(s). The neglect, the anger, and the emotional abandonment is not because you are bad, unlovable, or just not enough. You are not the problem, but unconsciously you take it on as yours. Too soon, the building blocks for your future prison foundations arrive.

Don Miguel Ruiz, in his insightful book, *The Four Agreements,* says, "That humans become domesticated."[3] Wild animals have the inborn skills and instincts to survive in the wild. Those who are raised in a controlled environment where food, shelter, and training are provided become dependent on others for their very survival.

They become domesticated. It is dangerous to set them free until they gain self-survival skills. As a young child, you literally cannot survive on your own. You are dependent upon adults to provide your survival needs. In human development, "domestication" is a natural and healthy stage.

It is when you have to do, say, and be something that goes against who you genuinely are, in order to ensure that your needs are met, that "domestication" becomes an early prison. John E. Bradshaw, author of *Homecoming*[4,] writes about the injured inner child. You-and all of us-remember injuries we sustained as children. The injuries of childhood that you carry into adulthood and that negatively impact the way you feel about yourself are the building blocks of your prison foundation. Here begins the accumulation of these building blocks to create an early "childhood fort," which later becomes an "adult prison." Ken Moses Ph.D.[5]

Building a fort of protection when you are a vulnerable child, and survival is the prime motivating force, makes perfect sense. As a young child, you have limited ability to create coping mechanisms and develop options. Anything that will allow you to survive and not go crazy is useful. What makes perfect sense to you as a child can make less sense when you become an adult. If you grow up in a physically abusive home, you might decide that you are to blame for the abuse you receive. You feel guilty because you have convinced yourself that you are so bad that your mother has to beat you. This guilt is really the child's protection against the harsh truth that your parent, the one you need for survival, is really the unhealthy one. To be aware of this would be too frightening. The problems begin when you don't let go of that early "fort" even though you now have the brain development to be aware of a variety of healthy and creative coping mechanisms. As an adult you continue to blame yourself and suffer guilt for the intolerable behavior on the part of another. Without awareness of the necessary switch, the fort becomes the prison. You have unwittingly become a Prison Builder.

In our self-created prison system, the prisons are often inter-locking. A prisoner who is in the *Prison of Perfection* could also inhabit the *Prison of Too Nice*. The *Prison of Fear of the Unknown* could house the same prisoner that is in the *Prison of Control*. One thing they all have in common is that they were built on founda-tions of survival and fear, and they were initially built for protection. Building a prison is a process, and the Prison Builder is the architect of that process. The building blocks for the foundation are gathered piece by piece, in reaction to perceived threats to survival. As you read this book you will start to bring consciousness to the process of prison building, a process that is usually unconscious. Since putting a name to something intangible makes it more knowable, we'll name each prison. The *reasons* you have for constructing each prison are the *building blocks* of that prison, reasons=building blocks and are gathered from stages of your personal life.

Although each prison is made of numerous building blocks, all prisons contain Foundational Building Blocks: Survival, Self-Protection, Fear, Limited Coping Skills, and a Need for Love. In this way, prisons are similar. The variations in each prison depend on how these Foundational Building Blocks are assembled. In reading the descriptions of the building blocks of a particular prison, you might find similarities to the building blocks of your personal pris-ons. If thirteen prisons are overwhelming, read through the names of each prison and first read those you relate to.

In the first Prison Builder Chapter we will take a "tour" of five Prisons:

- Prison of Rigidity

- Prison of Too Nice

- Prison of Guilt

- Prison of Worry

- Prison of Unhealthy Self-Judgment

PRISON OF RIGIDITY
(all or nothing; black or white)

This prison was built to protect you from the chaos in your life. You might live in a household where one parent works, or where both parents work. You could live in a household headed by a single parent or by other relatives. In any of these family configurations there was a lot of scheduling going on and a lot of vying for time. Schedules could get changed on a dime and the lack of consistency makes you feel unsafe and out of control. This chaotic environment that accompanied a busy family life was not necessarily what caused you to create your future Prison of Rigidity. The creation of this prison was from the *chaotic* behaviors and situations that frightened and confused you and made you feel out of control. As a child your brain was not developed enough to figure out why your parents often screamed at each other when everything seemed so okay, or why your mother was loving one day and withdrawn the next day. This erratic, chaotic behavior felt scary and very confusing. Your brain literally didn't have the ability to make sense out of the mixed signals, so you created a simple and consistent system to feel safe. You coped by telling yourself that everything was either right or wrong; that there was only one way to do something. The rigidity of this system (all or nothing; black or white) was your way of coping with the unsafe chaos, and it was effective. When you became an adult, life demanded flexibility, demanded the ability to live in the "grey area." If you remained rigid into adulthood, clinging to your old coping skill, you wound up in the Prison of Rigidity.

Building Blocks

Fear When you were little, the building blocks for the Prison of Rigidity started to arrive. You experienced the painful chaos around you. The chaos could have been due to:

- **Overextended caretakers**
- **Disorganized caretakers**
- **Inexperienced caretakers**
- **Inconsistent caretakers**
- **Frightening caretakers**
- **Absent caretakers**

You could have experienced some combination of the above caretakers, or all of them. Chaos created fear when your survival needs were threatened by that chaos. Perhaps your caretakers couldn't handle the numerous demands of being parent, partner, earner, home maintainer, sibling, and friend. These caretakers were *Overextended*. Their overextension created a chaotic environment that could have caused a caretaker to be *Disorganized* in caring for you. This disorganized caretaker could have been erratic in attending to your survival needs for food, physical care, and attention. You experienced being unsafe.

You could also have had *Inexperienced* caretakers. Most new parents are inexperienced and usually learn on the job. Courses on how to be a competent parent are not fully integrated into the educational system. Inexperience could have created chaos, and if, additionally, there was a lack of support, money, safety, and ability to multi-task, more chaos was created. If your caretaker was inconsistent, a level of chaos could have been created at which you felt unprotected and unloved. When your survival needs for protection and love were threatened, the prison building blocks piled up.

Frightening caretakers created a toxic chaos that made you instinctively build a fort of protection due to your limited coping skills. You would have blamed yourself for the abusive behavior of the caretaker in order to create clarity about who was right and who was wrong. This might have given you some sense of hope and control; if you changed your behavior the abuse would stop.

An *Absent* caretaker could also have been the source of the chaos you experienced in your home environment. The absent parent could have caused chaos by the void produced by his or her absence. Even if the absence was for the better, the change alone could have been unsettling. There are many factors that could have influenced chaos due to an absent caretaker: the cause of the absence; your age when the absence occurred; the reactions of the remaining caretakers; and the age-appropriate reasons given to you for the absence. If the absence wasn't allowed to be discussed, and your feelings therefore had no chance of being expressed, you would make up your own story and find a way with your limited coping skills to protect yourself from your fears. It was easier to blame yourself for the departure, even if it was a death, so you could bring clarity to the chaos of loss. You might have said to yourself, "I'm the reason Daddy left. If I stop being naughty, he will love me and no one will leave me again." This early protective rigidity of thought sets the stage for many future prisons, if it isn't reevaluated in adulthood.

Inconsistency Inconsistency is a large contributor to the building of this prison. You suffered from confusion over mixed messages received from your family. Members of your family said one thing, while doing another, taking actions that said the exact opposite of what was verbalized. This created an uncomfortable chaos in your mind and you had few coping mechanisms available to comfort yourself. As a very young child you were more attuned to actions, body language and tone. As you got older, the actions, as well as the words, were taken in to help you understand and sense what was happening in the environment. If you were told by your mother (in response to your nursery school teacher's call saying that you kept hitting Sarah), "You must be nice to everybody, you can't hit people," you were very confused because all you saw at home was your parents hitting each other and your siblings hit every day. You needed to find a way to protect yourself from the fear and discomfort that the inconsistency between words and actions in your family evoked in you. When this dissonance was continually repeated between what you were told and the actions you witnessed, the building blocks of your present fort and future Prison accumulated. It is important to mention at this point that your siblings, if you had any, might not have been affected in the same way. They may say they didn't think such and such even happened. If you ever ask yourself, "Did we grow up in the same family?" please remember to validate your own memories and feelings. They were real for you. They were so real that you created a fort, a chaos-busting fort that later became a Prison of Rigidity.

| Biological | Yet another building block of this prison could be biological. The way your brain processed information and stimuli could have contributed to an experience of chaos. The ability to process and integrate pieces of input might have operated, in your brain wiring, in a way that didn't protect you from the pain of fragmentation and confusion in the family environment. The pace of modern-day life, two or three after-school activities, and a busy home life went against your natural rhythm. If you had a slow...slow...

moderate...slow pace, and you lived in a household whose pace was fast...fast...fast, internal chaos could have been the result.

Remember, the Prison of Rigidity was a fort you used as a survival mechanism to lessen the pain of chaos. It was actually functional in that context. For the adult you, *rigidity, all or nothing, black or white* is limiting and imprisoning. The grey area is where a healthy life is lived.

PRISON OF TOO NICE

At an early age, many children are taught the "do's" and "don'ts" of being nice because it is a desirable personality trait. When, you might wonder, could nice, and especially "too nice" be anything but *positive*? When it is negative. Nice could be so negative, in fact, that it becomes imprisoning. Some children are taught at a young age that to survive, to be safe, and to be loved they must be nice. A young child has few coping mechanisms yet is smart enough to learn to use a behavior that gets needs met. The constant use of this behavior and the stress of not being able to risk showing any negative behaviors can be exhausting. The more being nice works, no matter what the emotional cost to that child, the more the child uses "nice." Somewhere along the line this behavior becomes automatic and unconscious. The foundational building blocks of the Prison of Too Nice have been laid.

Building Blocks

Validation You were directly taught the value of being nice to others. You got rewarded for being nice with verbal praise or with nonverbal approval. The reward could have been recognition through privileges or even through gifts. You were happy to get this validation for how nice you were and for all the nice things you did, so why then were you always frightened? You were frightened because you didn't believe that you could ever risk showing emotions that weren't so nice. You had to stuff down your feelings of anger and frustration when they bubbled up within you. At some point, you stopped exhibiting your own upsetness, fear, sadness, and anger. The next step was that you forgot you even had these feelings. You began to lose touch with how you honestly felt, and your confusion caused you constant anxiety. You were left with only one way to be: too nice.

Because you were convinced that your family would not like you, or even love you unless you were the 'nice one,' you were nice even when it wasn't appropriate. You told yourself you had no choice. You were now unconsciously controlled by the need for validation that this behavior afforded, never noticing the rising price you paid. It also frightened you to realize that you resented the role you now had to play in your family. The price you paid for validation was the price of admission into your self-built Prison of Too Nice.

Self-Protection You were a person who was sensitive to the feelings of your family members. You sensed when someone was upset, fearful, sad, or angry. You were also a person who was afraid of conflict. You tried to diffuse potentially hostile feelings between family members, or towards you, by being nice. When you were nice you reduced the possibility that you would incur the wrath of an angry or violent family member. When faced with a person who raged, a drunk, or someone who was downright mean, all the niceness in the world might not have saved you from abuse. But if being nice cut down on being singled out, even a few times, it was a valuable safety tool. You were the one who desperately needed to bring calm to the emotional environment. The need for self-protection at any cost was another building block for your Prison of Too Nice.

Need for Attention You had a busy home life. Every person in your household was vying for attention. You got attention when you were very nice. You were subtly taught that by being nice, you, — not your demanding siblings, —were given a few precious moments with your distracted mother. Not being nice evoked the words, "Be more like your sister; everybody says she's a pleasure," from your constantly traveling dad. You consciously realized that nice = attention. Being nice, as a method of getting the attention you needed, was the method you continued to use during your school years.

Your teachers loved you because you never caused any trouble and were always so very helpful. As an adult, you have now been unconsciously conditioned to be nice as a means of getting attention in your roles of employee, partner, and parent. Your time has become hard to manage, taken up by the increasing cast of characters you are attending to. It may be exhausting and/or time consuming, but the precious attention is worth the cost, until it isn't...but too late. Your need for attention has added still another set of building blocks to the Prison of Too Nice.

Need for Love You have, by this time, been labeled the nice one in the family (there could be worse labels). On the surface, this seems like a good thing, and it was until it became your expected role. You now do the dance of nice: you always listen, help, and choose others over yourself; you're sweet and cheery. Your family's part in this dance of too nice is to like you, to appreciate you, to praise you, and-most of all-to need and love you. You begin to notice that you aren't getting the same praise, attention, or love you need because it is taken for granted. You actually have to ramp up your niceness to get the old result. This is similar to needing more of a drug to get the same result you used to get from a lower dose.

The dance of *Too Nice* is a popular dance done in the *Prison of Too Nice* and it's exhausting.

PRISON OF GUILT AND WORRY
(Robbers of the Present)

The Prison of Guilt and Worry is the successor of one of the earliest childhood "fort's." The fort was built at the moment of your birth as a reaction to that first slap, as you entered this world. You felt guilty and asked yourself, "What did I do?" Could this unconscious reaction to the slap be original guilt? You started to worry about the future. You asked, "Will I ever feel as safe, as warm, or have my needs met as quickly as before that unexplainable slap?" These early forts were constructed before you became conscious of the power that guilt and worry have to imprison you throughout your life.

This is an old, expansive prison complex. To simplify, we will look at each of the two prisons in this complex individually, never forgetting that they are intricately intertwined. The building of the Prison of Guilt and the Prison of Worry was not based upon what happened in the past, or what might happen in the future. The building blocks were based upon *how you reacted to what happened.* Did you react with guilt about the past or worry about the future? Both reactions, especially when you were a child, stemmed from an unrealistic sense of responsibility, and an unrealistic assessment of your ability to be in control. Both reactions kept you from living in the present. Guilt and Worry literally became "Robbers of the Present."

PRISON OF GUILT

One definition of the noun *guilt* is "a feeling of responsibility or remorse for some offense, crime or wrong"--whether real or imagined."[6] The word guilt is found throughout religion, philosophy, law enforcement, and literature, in well-known phrases that describe guilt's many facets: guilt complex, guilt trip, collective guilt, existential guilt, inherited guilt, survivor's guilt, guilt by association, and presumption of guilt (just to name a few). The book *Guilt: The Bite of Conscience*, by Herant Katchadourian, looks at guilt across disciplines, religions, and philosophies. In his book, guilt is recognized as being both a healthy and an unhealthy response to life events.[7] As part of being alive you have expectations of yourself and others have expectations of you. Over your lifetime you are bound to fall short on occasion and respond to those unmet expectations with feelings of guilt: guilt for what you have or haven't done; guilt for what you do or don't feel; guilt for who you are or aren't. All these responses can be those of a person with a healthy conscience. Unhealthy guilt, the subject of this prison, develops when normal guilt morphs into a condemnation of self. When you fall short in any way, it becomes the grating voice in your head that keeps you in a past filled with guilty regrets. This unhealthy guilt is self-defeating and imprisoning.

Perhaps Eve felt guilty when she plucked the apple and fed it to Adam, but Shakespeare's King Macbeth not only felt guilt ridden, he was destroyed by his guilt. Guilt was and is a pervasive emotional reaction to life's events, and the Prison of Guilt is one that takes conscious, hard work to break out of. As a child, you liked to play with blocks: alphabet blocks, magnetic blocks, and Legos. These blocks were used as learning tools, as tools for the development of coordination, and just for fun. The building blocks for the Prison of Guilt, on the other hand, were piled high and used to help you survive, feel protected, feel loved, and lessen your fears. All this had to be done using your limited coping skills.

Building Blocks

Safety Your early world was, for the most part, small. It contained parents or a parent figure, siblings, and a few other people. Let's say that in your small world something went wrong. It could have been anything from a minor mishap to the seriousness of abuse. You needed to believe that the adults whom you depended upon for survival were able to meet your needs. You, the child, unconsciously figured out that, "If I'm to blame it's safer. Better it's me than the people I need to keep me safe." You blamed yourself as a protective coping mechanism against your fear, and at the same time you felt guilty. This limited, yet protective reasoning, "it's my fault," was a building block that was also used by you, the child, to create building blocks for the Prison of Rigidity. It was an interlocking prison system built block by block over many years.

Control On a less subtle level, you may have literally been told that if you were not better behaved, quieter, or more helpful, you would "kill your father or mother." Your behavior might cause one or the other to have a heart attack, and you could throw in a beloved grandparent for good measure. Oh boy! You sure are powerful for someone so little. These thoughtless statements made you feel responsible, and therefore guilty, when you were either misbehaving and noisy, or not so helpful. You were too young to say, "Excuse me, mother, this is an incorrect assessment of my behavior and responsibility." Instead you found the child's way to feel in control: you let yourself believe you were at fault. If you accepted that your behavior would be the cause of the death of your loved ones, then you could prevent their death by changing your behavior. The pain of guilt was worth the sense of control. The building blocks for the Prison of Guilt were piling up over your little head, and they kept on coming.

Approval Perhaps your earliest crime, for which you felt much guilt, was not having been the girl or the boy that was wanted. The silent disapproval you felt was a great threat to your need for approval and validation. Making up for that crime could take a lifetime and the guilt was your "gift" of apology. "My fault! My fault! I'll make it up to you; let me count the exhausting ways." The protective Fort of Guilt, precursor to the later Prison of Guilt, needed to be built. This self-assigned guilt was both protective and effective when survival was the goal. Your reaction of guilt at an early age was a learned response. It was reinforced by the all-important adults in your life and society, and by your Negative Self-Talk. Guilt was applied to many early situations in which you unfairly believed you fell short. You didn't do as you should have; you didn't behave as you should have; and you didn't feel as you should have. You as an adult are still piling on the guilt in situations in which you feel you have fallen short. You haven't done as well you should; you didn't behave as you should; and you haven't felt as you should. But remember, the emphasis of this book is not on the reasons you built your prisons. The emphasis of this book---- and its greatest value to you, the reader--- are the Keys that are available to unlock your prison doors.

PRISON OF WORRY

Worry is a necessary childhood fort, but it's one of the most pervasive, unnecessary, time-and-energy-draining adult prisons you can build. What are the building blocks for the Prison of Worry? They are blocks that ensure survival and protection against chaos and the unknown. The choice of blocks is as numerous as the number of unknowns in your future; infinite is the slightest exaggeration.

Building Blocks

Survival The building blocks for this Prison of Worry were clutched in your infant hands. As an infant, you were concerned about having your survival needs met. You were dependent upon others for food, for physical care, for a loving touch and for someone to hear your cries. These primal concerns, not yet identified as worry, were the seeds of all the worries to follow.

Fear of the Unknown In a home that sorely lacked any consistent routines, people, locations or behaviors, life was confusing and uncertain. What could you expect next? What could be known or counted on? The unknown could produce worry. The unknown, coupled with a minimum of coping skills, fueled this worry. You were now wired to worry in response to uncertainty. This wiring became reinforced when you were not kept informed by the adults in your life as to what to expect, and when the family kept everything secret. You were locked in a Prison of Worry when no one acknowledged your concerns and no one comforted you. A worry neural pathway in your brain was formed and strengthened. Since the unknown was so uncomfortable, you started to tell yourself stories about what might happen. You became a storyteller. You tried to make the unknown known, to fill in the gaps, and then you worried about the scary stories you created. Eventually you forgot you made up the stories. Your opportunities to worry increased. You could now worry about the unknown, and worry about the various stories you had created to lessen the stress of not knowing. Ironically, the stories only increased your stress and fortified the Prison of Worry. Guilt and Worry are part of everyone's life. Unearned guilt and unnecessary worry are imprisoning.

PRISON OF UNHEALTHY SELF-JUDGMENT

The Prison of Unhealthy Self-Judgment is built on self-blame. It is a multilayered prison whose bars block the prisoners from their compassionate and non-judging selves. Like every prison built, it offers a form of protection and safety, a form that by its very nature is imprisoning.

Building Blocks

Self-Protection A little blue or pink shovel was probably used early on to pile up blocks for this fort. You might have experienced numerous situations you didn't really understand and you had the uncomfortable sensation of being out of control. Now, in that little head of yours, you decided the situation was your fault. If it's your fault, if you're to blame, you are more in control. At least you knew whose fault it was. Maybe if you could do better, be better, or behave better, the situation would be better. Your Unhealthy Self-Judgment "(it's my fault)" actually makes you feel safer. Some of these same building blocks were used in the Prison of Rigidity and the Prison of Guilt. Many prison builders use the same blocks for different prison constructions. Most prisons have blocks found elsewhere in this vast prison system.

Need for Safety In your family of origin you might have been assigned the unspoken role of scapegoat. More than likely it was your fault when the baby woke up, when something broke, when mommy or daddy was mad, or when the sun didn't shine. It was hard to understand why this assignment occurred; for you it was impossible to understand. It created in you the intensely uncomfortable sensations of chaos, fear, and guilt. You needed to get rid of these sensations that made you feel unsafe. One way to do this was to make an Unhealthy Self-Judgment, and to blame yourself in order to bring clarity and safety to the chaos of not knowing. The people you needed were not crazy; they didn't have poor judgment, and they didn't dislike you. They were okay and you were safe in their care. Your coping mechanism was to tell yourself that you were to blame; it was your fault; you were not okay. What a relief!

There was no shortage of material for this thick-walled prison. Building upon the scapegoat experience, you the adult have now internalized the role of "the one who is to blame." Even though it remains extremely painful to be judged in this way, as the one who is always at fault, you have picked up the baton and become the self-blamer. The Prison of Unhealthy Self-Judgment has taken shape. Believe it or not, it is less painful to blame yourself than to wait for those you love to blame you, yet again. Protection, protection, protection is the prison's *raison d'être*. Both consciously and unconsciously, you have accepted that you're not enough.

Now you start to look for situations and for people who will reinforce this self-judgment. You set undoable goals. You find people (and there's a large pool to pick from) who need to blame someone else. You stop trying to do things. Why? You don't do anything right anyway. You are in the prison of Unhealthy Self-Judgment because you turned yourself in. You know you did it!

Self-assessment, not judgment, is an important tool in self-development. Those who use *self-assessment* are not to be found in this prison system. They have learned how to make honest, non-judging assessments based on thoughtful questions, and how to take a healthy step back for a broader perspective of themselves. They hold some of the Keys to be found in the Key Holder section of this book.

Prisoner Builder Role-Prison Builder

Put a check next to the prisons you might have built:

- **Prison of Rigidity** ____

- **Prison of Too Nice** ____

- **Prison of Guilt** ____

- **Prison of Worry** ____

- **Prison of Unhealthy Self-Judgment** ____

CHAPTER FIVE

More Prisons

In this second Prisoner Builder chapter we will 'visit' four prisons.

- **The Prison of Perfection**
- **The Prison of-Fear-of-the Unknown**
- **The Prison of Control**
- **The Prison of Unhealthy Patterns**

Perhaps one of these four prisons seems familiar. Read through the building blocks used for each prison and ask yourself, "Have I used these blocks, or similar blocks, to construct my prison? Could I still be in this prison?" You can't break out of any prison until you're aware that you're in it.

PRISON OF PERFECTION

This prison could also be called the Prison of Impossible Dreams. The material for its construction is always on order because this prison is never finished; it is never good enough. Often these prisoners are serving a life sentence. They are so busy editing life that they forget they haven't gone before the parole board. Trying to be perfect is exhausting and anxiety producing. To reduce their constant feeling of anxiety these prisoners have also built the Prison of Control. They divide their time between these two formidable structures.

Building Blocks

Safety You were born into a family that had a unique structure and way of interrelating. At some early age you figured out, perhaps unconsciously, that if you did everything perfectly you wouldn't draw attention to yourself. You noticed that attention, in this family, was not a good thing. Because you didn't cause any trouble, no one paid attention to you. You could do it all yourself and do it perfectly. Your perfection gave you a cloak of invisibility. It also gave you the anxiety that accompanies the need to always be perfect.

Need for Love Perhaps you were born into a family where you were shown love if you got an A++ on a paper in school. In this family, you desperately wanted to be noticed so you studied hours and hours to achieve this coveted grade; and you achieved it. You were only shown love if you looked impeccable. You did look impeccable and you spent hours and hours to look that way. Or you were shown love if you won the contest that would do your family proud. You did win the contest, after spending hours and hours figuring out how to win it. To win the title of Little Miss Perfect or Little Mister

Perfect you had to try very hard to be perfect, because you believed you were flawed and imperfect.

Need for Control Perfection was an unhealthy form of control. It was your coping mechanism because you had a limited choice of coping mechanisms. You felt more in control when trying to make something perfect. You felt more in control when "changing someone" to make that person perfect. You thought if you put more time and attention into what or whom you were trying to perfect, you could effect the changes you needed to. Then you could be more certain that things would be better, that a relationship would be better, that life would be better and more knowable. Your young child's brain was undeveloped and couldn't handle abstract reasoning and other higher functions of the pre-frontal lobe. This part of your brain was still under development until your early twenties. This biological factor, coupled with the natural uncertainty caused by new people and new experiences, made your early life unknowable. Being perfect, your method of control, was your coping mechanism for handling this unknowable world. When not modified in adulthood, it became imprisoning. Recognizing a need for improvement and taking action was healthy, but the Prison of Perfection was built upon not knowing when it was healthy to stop trying to control situations and people around you.

Fear of Failure/of Success Another reason you might have built this Prison of Perfection was due to the underlying fear of either failure or of success. Your time-consuming striving for perfection, which looked noble on the surface, was a great avoidance technique. How could you complete a project, bring an idea, painting, or book to fruition, when it was never quite right? One more dab of green, one more revision of chapter two, one more... Striving for perfection became the focus and the goal was forgotten. You never had to face your fear of success or failure. Perfect.

The building blocks for this prison piled up when you continually reached for an elusive perfection in yourself or in others. You reached for this even though there was solid proof that something about you, or someone that meant a lot to you, couldn't change in the way that you needed.

Is striving for excellence commendable? It is. It is, until that excellence becomes perfection—the only outcome that you use as proof of your worth. It is, until the search for perfection keeps you from your need for completion, and until it starts to control your life.

Control is a word that rears its head in the building blocks of many prisons. We'll visit the Prison of Control right after we visit the Prison of Fear of the Unknown, control's nemesis.

PRISON OF FEAR OF THE UNKNOWN

Little can really be known. This inability to know causes fear. The unknown is an infinite land. No one knows what will happen in the next ten minutes of your life, let alone next year. This prison, is large and overcrowded with prisoners. Who hasn't been faced with a decision that requires a substantial change, maybe a change of job, or of location, or even of a relationship? The decision not to make the change is often due to the fear of the unknown. The big dark abyss of the unknown is so frightening that perhaps you choose to stay imprisoned in a job, in a location, or even in a relationship that is no longer healthy. You become imprisoned by the fear of the unknown.

Because so many of the prisons you'll read about are interwoven with the Prison of the Fear of the Unknown they become part of an interdependent prison system. The unknown causes great anxiety for those in the prison you have just visited, the Prison of Perfection. Fear of the unknown is the main reason so many of us build the Prison of Worry. The prisoners in the Prison of Control, our next prison visit, shutter at its mere name...*UNKNOWN*. Many prisoners have built and inhabited several, if not all, of the prisons in this system.

Building Blocks

Protection This prison, like so many others, starts as a necessary and protective fort. Your world as an infant and toddler is fraught with the unknown. Once again, your early survival needs make you scream for attention. The unknown…Will you be heard? Will you be fed? Will you be safe and cared for? When these needs are not met, especially if they are regularly not met, the unknown becomes associated with risk to survival, and with a sense of fear.

Acceptance When you enter a school system, there are rules and expectations for the student, and the unknown looms: Are you able to adhere to the rules? Are you able to meet the expectations? If you are actually unable, for any of a myriad of reasons, to adhere to the structure of the rules, if unable to meet the rhythm of the school day, or unable to follow instructions the way they are delivered, you may begin to fear unknowns even more. The Prison of Fear of the Unknown now has a new environment from which to get inmates… school.

Clarity Teens inhabit a world that changes minute by minute. The changes are all encompassing, affecting the mental, physical and social aspects of his being. When you are a teen, how your body will look, let alone feel, is unknown and can be frightening. This is less so now, with sex and health education. If you were born at a time when these vital topics weren't part of a curriculum, or your parents were uncomfortable imparting this information, or you didn't have close friends, questions such as, "What is happening to me?" and "What are these 'funny' feelings?" might not get answered. More unknowns. In "the old days" some young girls might have gone into the bathroom one day and thought they were bleeding to death, or young boys might have woken up from a wet, sticky dream, not understanding, only terribly ashamed. Funny? Not at the time. The unknown. "What will happen to me next?" Every aspect of your life at this stage is unclear. The lack of clarity you experience on a daily basis as a teenager, reinforces your Fear of the Unknown.

Change Emotions can feel like a scary roller coaster ride. They are uncomfortable and unknown to the teen feeling them. The pull to grow up and be your own person is only matched by the pull to have your parents meet your needs and the pull to be just like those in your peer group. If you don't ask yourself, "What's wrong with me?" others might ask in other words: "What did you do to your hair?" "What are you wearing?" "Is that a tattoo?" "You pierced what?" "Who were you with?" "What's wrong with you?" Unknowns abound. How the teen approaches the unknowns and if others help or hinder will lessen the fear or add fuel to it. The Prison Fear of the Unknown gets its inmates from yet another environment… the teenage years.

Now you are an adult. No more fear of the unknown to imprison you, right? Wrong! The unknowns lie in wait at every turn. So many choices need to be made before you are ready to make them and to know what would be right for you. You have to decide whether to take the path to higher education, the path directly to work, or the path that leads to a combination of both. When you are forced to make this choice at age sixteen, seventeen, eighteen, or nineteen, the best path for you can't be known. The best choice for you, a "you" that is barely formed at this early age, is a scary unknown. Should you do the type of work many members of your family trained for, or just wound up doing? Should you enlist in the armed services like so many in your family before you? Should you date, live with, or marry a particular person? Where should you live? What can you know at this time of your life when so many import-ant, and perhaps life-changing, decisions are thrust upon you? That all-encompassing Prison of Fear of the Unknown, makes room in your cell for an ever-changing environment: LIFE.

PRISON OF CONTROL

The Prison of Control is built on a shaky foundation. The foundation is shaky because it is built on the condition of "not enough." It was built by the very young child having "not enough" coping skills needed for survival. "Not enough" trust—primarily lack of self-trust—then lack of trust of others. As in many other prisons, the building blocks for the Prison of Control are gathered early. Some gathering was done unconsciously, and at some point a conscious gathering was added to the mixture. Control is an ever-changing entity. One can take control, be in control, be under control, be out of control, or be a control freak. There is a form of control, which, paradoxically, causes you to be controlled by your need for control, and that is the cement of this prison.

Building Blocks

Survival As an infant or young child you might have cried out when you were hungry, tired, afraid, or confused. No one responded, or they took too long to respond. You had no other way to call attention to your needs. Your cries escalated and you felt you had no control over getting your basic needs met. You were given the message, through actions or words, "to control yourself." These words and accompanying tone and body language were repeated each time you cried out. Methods of control for someone so young are limited. Survival is the real mother of invention. What was adaptive when you were very young (rocking yourself, stuffing a hand or blanket in your mouth not to cry out, suffering the discomforts of body, mind and spirit in silence) was the beginning of this adult prison.

Self-Protection As your world got bigger and included school, teachers, playmates and classmates, your unconscious awareness of how little you controlled was countered by your conscious effort to exert control; your need for control became inversely proportional to your lack of control. Using limited coping mechanisms, you developed methods to control the anxiety of not having enough control. You may have developed some rituals that made you feel more in control. You started to wear something that you deemed "lucky" when you had any important decision to make. You started to use a certain pen when taking a test. You traveled only on Tuesdays, your "lucky" day, to ensure a safer flight.

Superstitions have evolved as a way to feel in control. They have been passed down through generations of those who dwell in the Prison of Control. These time-honored superstitions once were performed for a genuine purpose. With that original purpose now forgotten, they serve only as an illusion of protection, as a way to feel safe and as a way to control "fate." A wonderful story illustrates this point. This story, had been told in a variety of forms. I'm recounting the way I remember it being told to me.

A young woman was making a roast for her family. Before she put it in the pot, she cut several inches off the roast at one end. Her teenage daughter asked her why she did this. Surprised that her daughter was paying any attention, the woman admitted she didn't know. She decided to call her mother, who always did the same thing. Her mother was also perplexed about this family method of preparing a roast. She in turn called her own ninety-five-year-old mother. About twenty minutes later, the young woman, a granddaughter in this line of women, was still in the kitchen with her mother when the phone rang. Her mother answered the phone, listened, and burst out laughing.

"What! What?" her daughter demanded, "Your great-grandmother cut inches off her roasts... because her pan was too small. I do it as the only way to ensure my roast will be perfect!"[8]

Need to Change Others Until you realize, if you ever do, that you cannot control other adults, you will continually try to. Although frustrating at best, the trying might still feel better to you than consciously acknowledging that you have no control over your loved ones. You have probably said or heard, "If he was my boyfriend, if she was my girlfriend, friend, he would say this, she would do this, he would want this." If only you could give the people you love your script for them! "My child is really smart. Her difficulties at school are just laziness. Our family goes to college." The unspoken monologue is, "This is the right path for my child, a member of our family and representative of my family unit." The futile attempt at control goes on. "I'll put him on a diet and we'll join the gym. I'll keep sugar out of the house. It will work this time." "I know this is just a very stressful year. Her drinking helps her relax. I really won't let her drive next time. How can I help reduce her stress? I'll think of some way." The more you feel out of control, the more controlling you become. People start screaming, or whispering behind your back, "Control freak." You have become controlled by your need for control.

The building blocks for this ubiquitous prison keep piling up. If only this industrious prison builder would read the wisdom imparted in the Serenity Prayer, by Reinhold Niebuhr, "God grant me the serenity to accept the things I cannot change; courage to change the things I can; and the wisdom to know the difference." [9]

Life happens. We can plan. We can take healthy actions to complete the plans, and life still happens. The outcome is not in your control. The Prison of Control is filled with those who keep insisting that life, and all those in it, follow a path they envision. If this is true for you, go directly to the Prison of Control and don't collect $200.00.

PRISON OF UNHEALTHY PATTERNS

Some patterns are followed in order to make things, from clothes to buildings, based on healthy foresight. These are not the patterns that make up the Prison of Unhealthy Patterns.

The patterns that sentence you to this prison are those that formed early and were protective. The patterns became unhealthy and imprisoning when not consciously reexamined as they repeated throughout your life. You need to ask yourself, "Are these patterns contributing to a healthy life, or are they imprisoning me in a never-ending repetition of unhealthy interactions?"

Building Blocks

Safety of the Familiar You form patterns of interaction with other people. These patterns could be called dances. You dance together and you each have your own steps that you learn to do in this interactive dance. The steps get repeated until they are learned, then memorized, and then finally internalized. Your family has its dance; a repetitious pattern with assigned steps. Each knows their part. As years go on the music may change, the people may change, but your steps remain the same. The pattern, the original family dance, though unhealthy, is perpetuated.

Patterns that are started very early can begin to define you. This is the pattern of behavior that others now expect of you. The expectations strengthen the behaviors and the pattern is reinforced. When you were young you might have been labeled "the cute one," or "the clumsy one," or "the funny one," or "the smart one," or "the sick one," or "the responsible one," or "the late one," and so on. These labels got attached to you by others and then by yourself. Eventually, these behaviors became the unhealthy patterns that define you. You still carry these patterns with you wherever you go.

Acceptance In school you are now that "the cute one," "the clumsy one," "the smart one," and you have the pressure to remain so, to continue the family dance. You are already imprisoned in these patterns. You don't pay attention to that knowing inner voice that says, "You're not clumsy when you're not so nervous. You have grace," or, "Yes you're cute, but you're also smart, and funny," or, "Yes you're smart, but you're allowed to make mistakes and don't always have to do better than everyone else. Relax."

Perhaps you are Johnny, who has always been labeled "the late one." Everybody knows this and expects you to be late. You have, over time, honed behaviors that contribute to your inability to be on time. Even when a friend gets angry because he or she misses the beginning of a game, show, or meeting, waiting for you to be ready, you continue your pattern of being late and unreliable. Even when your new boss has already talked to you for the second time in a month about being late, you continue this pattern. You know yourself as "Johnny Come Lately," the name given to you fondly, or not so fondly, by those who know you.

Your unexamined early patterns are the material of this Prison of Unhealthy Patterns. You follow a pattern in the people you choose to have in your life. Did you ever have a close friend say, "Don't you see, he fits your pattern of picking emotionally distant men?" or "She's just like your last two exes, so clingy." Why would you consciously repeat unhealthy patterns? You wouldn't! You're unconscious. You're already armed with your internalized steps from your family's dance. You're looking for people who know the steps your family members took so you don't have to learn a new dance.

True, this dance might not be danced at a comfortable pace for you, or in a style that fits your natural style. It might not even allow for your genuine rhythm, but it has the allure of the familiar.

Until you recognize that the dance is an unhealthy pattern, you will continue to find the people who will perpetuate it and help you stay locked in the Prison of Unhealthy Patterns.

Prisoner Builder Role-More Prisons

Put a check next to the prisons you might have built:

- **The Prison of Perfection** ____
- **The Prison of Fear of the Unknown** ____
- **The Prison of Control** ____
- **The Prison of Unhealthy Patterns** ____

CHAPTER SIX

No End To Prisons

The last four prisons we will visit are:

- **The Prison of Anger**
- **The Prison of Victimhood**
- **The Prison of Shame** (a very large prison complex)
- **The Prison of Avoidance of Pain.**

These prisons are well known for containing many chambers for solitary confinement. Reputedly, they do not need prison guards. The self-torturing nature of the prisoners is all that is needed to keep them confined. Do any of these prisons sound familiar?

PRISON OF ANGER

Anger is an emotion. The dictionary defines it as "a strong feeling of displeasure and belligerence aroused by a real or supposed wrong; wrath; ire."[10] Anger can be freeing, or it can be imprisoning. Healthy anger, to my mind, was best expressed by Aristotle in the *Nicomachean Ethics*, ten books, originally scrolls, that addressed how men should best live. "Anyone can become angry—that is easy. But to be angry with the right person, to the right degree, at the right time, for the right purpose, and in the right way—this is not easy."[11] Healthy anger is not easy.

Healthy anger is *not* the anger that is expressed by the inmates in the Prison of Anger. Anger that imprisons begins as a Protective Fort. It morphs into imprisoning anger when it is modeled after inappropriate displays of anger in your early home life. It is imprisoning when it is used to cover more painful emotions, and when it is used to intimidate others and distance yourself. This anger starts to keep you from getting what you want most, or getting it at the cost of others. This anger, over time, can create a self-loathing which makes you a perfect inmate in the red hot Prison of Anger.

Building Blocks

Early Predisposition You may have entered this world with a propensity to be quick to anger. You may have low impulse control, a function of the pre-frontal cortex. Adding to that is your knee-jerk response to anger, which is honed in the amygdala, a primitive part of our brain. It takes about 90 seconds for anger's neural firings to reach the more reasoned neo-cortex. This is when you are able to make a choice about your reaction.

When you are a child, it can be difficult to wait the 90 seconds for the tempering of the neo-cortex. If your brain is wired for impulsivity, to wait is especially difficult. Children are not known for their patience. "Are we there yet?" is a classic example. If no one is present to diffuse the many frustrations you encounter, especially if you are wired with low impulse control, anger as a response becomes a pattern that is reinforced each time you act it out.

Learned Behavior As a child you are an observant sponge and able mimic. This combination lets you take in the interactions, tones, behaviors, facial expressions, and body language of the family members in your small universe. You see, and perhaps store on a conscious or unconscious level, cause and effect. For example, someone does something wrong (cause) and Mom screams (effect). Dad comes home late for the umpteenth time(cause)and mom screams (effect). Mom forgets to do X (cause)and Dad's face is stern; he points a finger; the energy in the room is charged (effect). You, the child, are taking in the modeled reactive behavior. This anger is now normal in your world. At this age you aren't a generator of options, so you learn anger is "the way."

Self-Protection As you enter the broader world of school, new relationships are formed. You now interact with teachers (new authority figures), classmates, and the larger student population. Your genetic temperament, brain wiring, and learned anger responses are now transferred to this school environment. You use anger in the classroom as the only way to relieve frustration, and to intimidate others as a means of protection.

When you have too much difficulty with a lesson, you might angrily act out the pain of frustration. You might even rage, or throw a fit. When a classmate says something hurtful to you, or excludes you from a group, you might lash out and intimidate this classmate by aggressive body language, tone of voice, or the finger pointing you witnessed at home. Soon you are labeled "the angry one," and classmates keep their distance.

Teachers talk to you about your behavior and to your parents, who get angry with you for being angry. If there isn't a healthy intervention at this point, anger as a response, a weapon, and a form of protection, becomes a pattern. If it is not modified by the time you reach adulthood, anger imprisons you.

Ingrained Behavior In your teenage years, if no one has helped you find healthier means of coping or healthier ways to express anger, you might now be a "rebel without a cause." Anger is expected, anger is who you are, and anger gets you what you want. Who cares at what cost? Add substances to this established reaction and the anger could become explosive, leaving no room for thought or choice. The dance of anger whirls out of control...others beware. Relationships might develop with people unhealthy enough to tolerate the intolerable. Anger is no longer a protection and control; rather, it controls you and imprisons you in a world made smaller by the losses it inflicts.

If anger is now your ingrained response, the adult world is fraught with opportunities to respond with it. The dance of anger in your family of origin continues and it is a training ground for all future relations. In a disagreement with friends, you win by intimidation. Eventually, no one bothers to disagree. This may look like winning, but in reality all honest relating has ended and conversations become more and more limited. Those that stay in the friendship might use lies when they fear the truth will "set you off." Friends that seek more honest and relaxed interactions begin to fade away. The losses continue.

Your romantic interactions trigger you to the angry responses you witnessed between your parents. Your anger keeps you distanced from your partner. Your anger limits communications that could promote better understanding. It erodes trust, erodes respect and can do fatal damage to healthy love. Your old Protective Fort of anger is now imprisoning. You are now in the Prison of Anger. On visiting day, no one comes.

PRISON OF VICTIMHOOD

For victimhood to exist, there must be a victim and a victimizer. As a child, you can be a victim. The victimizer takes advantage of your vulnerability, dependence, and fearfulness. You have limited coping skills or options to adequately protect yourself from the experience of victimhood. Victimizers prey on those less powerful. They need someone to have control over, someone who they can unleash their frustrations on. Who better than a small, helpless person who can't fight back?

Perhaps you were not a victim in your home. Your childhood was "good enough," if not better. Not all physical responses are abusive. A tap on the bottom can help a child remember not to run into the street again. Not all yelling is abusive. In some families, it's the normal mode of communication, mixed with hand gestures and laughter. But all sexual treatment of a child, from looks, language, touching, to sexual acts is abusive. Abuse victimizes the helpless child.

Even if you weren't victimized as a child, could you "play" the role of victim as an adult? Yes. You could observe and absorb information that shows you the "benefits" of being a victim.

Building Blocks

Self-Protection You may have had the great misfortune to grow up in an environment where you were genuinely victimized. Why were you victimized? Whatever the "rationale" of the victimizers, their own history, their addictions, their temperament, their needs, or their life circumstances, it had nothing to do with you. Let me repeat: *it had nothing to do with you*. You were just there, helpless and probably needing love. You did not even know the word victim. But the feelings it produced—fear for survival, chaos, sadness, loneliness, anger, and helplessness—were known to you, sometimes on a daily basis. The painful experience of being a victim was very real, and very damaging. Due to the severity of the victimization, you were traumatized. Your body absorbed this trauma, storing it deep within your cells. Your senses became permeated by the victimization, ready to be triggered by a certain sound, sight, smell, taste, or touch. Your young child's mind had limited ability to modify and process information. Hurtful treatment = it's your fault. At this age, you aimed the blame at yourself. Self-blame was a fort of protection that began as a defensive weapon but later became a weapon against yourself.

Acceptance | A continuation of victimhood could have been fueled by the prejudices of the people in your country of origin; the social culture of the time; the makeup of your neighborhood; and the prejudice of your own extended family system. A sense of victimhood could have been deepened by these family prejudices: prejudice toward your gender; toward your sexual orientation; toward your appearance; or toward ways you were physically or mentally different. To be victimized is never good. To be victimized because of who you essentially were by birth, not who you were by the sum of your choices, is deeply painful. If you later challenged this treatment, the Prison of Victimhood wouldn't be built. If it was not challenged, and this imposed victimhood was accepted by you and acted upon, it became the building blocks for the Prison of Victimhood.

Fear | You now entered the school system a victim, a victim by early training at the hands of your victimizers. You drew to you the kids that had a "victim detector." You got in their space and the detector went "beep, beep, beep." They knew whom to attack; you were the turtle who lost its shell, the snake who shed its skin, the kid who entered a scary new system, vulnerable and without the skills of healthy self-protection.

The middle school years could put notches on the belt of victimhood, even for those without an early indoctrination. It was in the school years that victimhood's weapon, *blame*, changed your focus from yourself to others. Did the cumulative pain of being a victim become so great that your usual defense, "It's my fault," no longer served to make you feel protected? Now, "It's your fault, you are to blame," felt more protective. Though acceptance by your peer group might have been very important to you, it was not the life-or-death dependency on your family of origin. You could afford to think your peers were wrong. The criteria for feeling protected were switched. You now felt protected by being right, by being "the wronged one," yet again. You needed to boost your trampled ego, so when you asked yourself, "What's wrong with me? Why can't I get what or who I want? Why is my life so miserable?" the answer was, "Nothing's wrong with me. It's their fault. I'm a victim." This thinking was the new source of comfort and safety. The finger of blame turned outward. The prison doors slammed shut!

Attention You began to use the word "victim," whose meaning you had memorized, to describe who you were. It was how you saw yourself, and how you portrayed yourself to anyone who would listen. The world responded to this portrayal. You discovered, consciously or unconsciously, that there were "benefits" to being a victim. Some people felt sorry for you. You were the codependent's delight. Some people paid attention to you. Some people supported your story of how bad things always were for you. You convinced them and yourself that you were unable to be, unable to do, unable to have. This was no longer the child who was victimized. This was the adult you not stepping into your power, the adult you not making conscious choices. Not making the conscious choice to be a "victim no more." You were in a prison that needed very few jailors. This prison had become too comfortable to leave, because while you were in it, you were responsible for nothing!

PRISON OF SHAME

Many imprisoned in the Prison of Shame spend much of their incarceration in the prison hospital. These are deeply wounded prisoners. It is not uncommon for them to be transferees from the Prison of Anger and the Prison of Guilt. The Prison of Guilt and The Prison of Shame are not the same. Inmates in the Prison of Guilt are imprisoned because of their extreme guilt over what they've done. The Prison of Shame holds inmates who are deeply ashamed of who they are. The Prison of Shame is always built at the deepest level of the prison structure. It oozes pain from every cell. It is a prison that needs many keys to open its well-fortified door.

Building Blocks

Self-Protection You weren't born ashamed. You were born knowing the wonder of your being. You were a miracle. But sometime early on, you were given a message, by words, or by actions. You might have heard, "Shame on you" or "You should be ashamed of yourself." Either way, the message was that your "being" was not okay. This message went deeper than a criticism of your behavior. It was a damaging critique of your essence. This created the painful experience of shame. Again, it was not about what you did, but about who you were. At this stage, it was really about others and their dysfunctions. Since conscious reasoning was not available to you yet, you unconsciously absorbed these pronouncements as truth, and the seed of shame was embedded. Through the years this seed was watered, first by others, and then by you. It sprouted into a complex prison system. The Prison of Shame and the Prison of Avoidance of Pain, our next prison visit, housed the same prisoners. This early embedded shame was worn like a cloak. This cloak, rather than protecting you, acted as a barrier to your healthy being. When in school halls, you walked huddled, always carrying shame's burden. You pulled into yourself and tried for invisibility. You rarely stood up for yourself because you didn't feel you had any rights. You didn't deserve better treatment.

The kids smelled blood and tried to embarrass someone so easily embarrassed. They excluded someone already invisible. Their treatment added to the isolation that shame invited; isolation not wanted on the one hand, yet sought after on the other. Always feeling ashamed of yourself, you rarely tried for what you wanted. You rarely tried for what your innate interests and abilities would allow you to have achieved. It was hard for you to speak out or to speak up when you were always hiding. This failure, by default, added to your sense of shame, and the cycle continued.

You might not have joined the teams you had the skill to play on, taken electives that would have furthered your interests, or talked to classmates you were attracted to and would have liked to know. You wore your shameful cloak and it blocked all the opportunities available to the other children, who were not behind bars in the Prison of Shame during their school years. As an adult, this early, unchallenged shame continued to hold you back. Every life choice was influenced by your sense of worthlessness. At work and in your personal relationships, you were drawn to blamers and shamers. They were the partners in your old dance of shame. Shame was exhausting. It caused havoc on the body, mind, and spirit. It took no holiday. Shame was a monster that fed upon an early untruth and kept the emotional pain at high pitch. It was such a high level of pain that few had the courage to come out of hiding and challenge the life-sucking monster. The Prison of Shame was well guarded from within its multilayered walls.

PRISON OF AVOIDANCE OF PAIN

There is no greater pain, than the pain of avoiding pain.

The prisoners in the thirteenth prison never read the above phrase; if they did, they had no sense of its meaning. The inmates here have a credo: avoid pain at all costs. And they did. The cost was astronomical. "How do I avoid pain? Let me count the ways." Remember that the child's "Fort," avoidance of pain, was a protective structure. Even as an adult, at times, pain was so overwhelming that your mind and body needed the "break" of denial or other momentary means of avoidance because you couldn't safely take in the unbearable situation. Sometimes, avoidance was truly the best choice because you couldn't change the situation or accept it. Healthy avoidance was a temporary solution and not one that imprisoned.

Building Blocks

Survival We all have different levels of pain tolerance, both emotional and physical, but when pain exceeds your tolerance level, something needs to be done. As an infant you had no options. As a young child your options were limited. If you were in a family that inflicted physical or emotional pain, finding ways to avoid this continued unbearable pain was a survival goal. You might have tried to be as quiet as possible, even hide so as not to be noticed. You might have self-soothed by sucking your thumb, rocking yourself, and even singing to yourself.

As you got older, you might have lied to avoid retribution, or pointed a figure at another. When the pain became too great you might have dissociated, looked upon yourself as a separate entity to put distance between you and the emotional and physical abuse. The connection between avoidance as an action, and less pain as a result, became unconsciously embedded. The "Fort of Avoidance of Pain" was your only protection.

Normal pain was part of a normal life. Unbearable pain overshadowed normal pain. Protecting yourself from unbearable pain through avoidance created a pattern of avoidance in response to any pain. This pattern kept you from learning a variety of ways to handle life's regular pains. All levels of pain were filed under the heading "something to avoid." You then entered the school years without the skill to handle life's normal pain.

Control School life was fraught with little pains. You might have experienced disappointments, embarrassments, and perceived failures. You transferred your self-taught pain reliever to this new environment. You might have avoided others, stayed quiet and remained alone in the classroom, in the hallways, in the cafeteria, and in the schoolyard. "Avoid" was your unconscious credo. By this method you might have missed the kidding, the teasing, the pushing, and being called on in class. You were safe but you missed the chance to learn how to handle, and to make tolerable, the kidding, teasing, pushing, and being called on in class. You missed the joy of being a kid in school, the joy of learning and overcoming, and the joy of connection. In these early school years, denial, lies and hiding were still your only means of avoiding pain. These became the building materials for your future prison.

Anesthetize In the teenage years, and sadly often before then at nine, ten, eleven, or twelve years old other methods of avoiding pain became known to you. They were modeled in your peer group and they were available. These new methods might have been modeled in your family of origin but the connection was not yet made. You were unaware that they were methods of pain avoidance. These new methods were really just a more advanced development of your early thumb sucking, rocking and self-singing. Substances, the fuel of addictions, entered the scene. Addictions were a new multilayered cloak under which to hide, a protection gone awry. These were the dysfunctional "coping skills" that gave meaning to the insightful phrase: *There is no greater pain than the pain of avoiding pain.*[12]

Safety If by the time you entered the adult years, you hadn't developed other means of handling pain, the prison of Avoidance of Pain locked you into a world of isolation. It was a world where intimacy was restricted by the overwhelming need for the safety of distance. A distance from life's problems and from the people connected to those problems. There was no distinction between levels of pain. If pain was a component of a situation, a relationship, an internal stirring, then avoidance was the practiced reaction, the singular coping method. Avoidance created a void that you could spend your life trying to fill.

* * *

The thirteen Prisons described in the Prison Builder chapters might have a familiar ring. The building blocks used in constructing a prison, or several prisons, might have been blocks you used to construct your life prisons. Not until you are conscious that you are imprisoned will you begin to search for, and find, the keys you need for your joyous prison break.

Prison Builder Role-No End To Prisons

Put a check next to the prisons you might have built:

- The Prison of Anger _____

- The Prison of Victimhood _____

- The Prison of Shame _____

- The Prison of the Avoidance of Pain _____

Part III

Jailer Role

CHAPTER SEVEN

Jailers

Jailers come in all shapes and sizes, all races and religions, and all ethnicities. Although Jailers can be different in many ways, they have one universal trait. *They lack awareness.* They are actually unconscious! They have no clue, or maybe just an inkling, that they are experienced Jailers. This is the reason you can be both Prisoner and Jailer. You play the role of Jailer so unconsciously that you are genuinely unaware you keep yourself imprisoned. Your job as Jailer is to keep you Prisoner, in that well-built prison because you deserve to be imprisoned. Yet every now and then, when the prison is quiet, the Jailer will look over at the prisoner and get a momentary feeling of connection and familiarity.

The prison itself, its very construction in these quiet hours is uncannily familiar. As quickly as these feelings come, they pass, and you the Jailer once again sees you the Prisoner as separate from yourself, and the prison as a structure built by strangers.

The Jailer is always vigilant in making sure the prisoner remains confined. The Jailer is unaware that he is also the person who repeatedly reminds the Prisoner of how deserving s/he is of being imprisoned. As if these responsibilities were not enough, the Jailer makes sure the prison building itself remains strong and impenetrable.

The resume format is used to give you more information about the Jailer role you unconsciously play. The resumes were created to approximate what potential Jailers would have submitted if they were conscious and realized that they were highly qualified applicants.

Unconsciousness is the life-breath of a Jailer. Bringing consciousness to the job of Jailer is the first and perhaps the most important step toward the extinction of this job. As you read each resume, especially the *personal characteristics* and the *special skills*, see if you get a sense of whether you, too, might possess some of the Jailer traits and skills. This awareness, if approached as a Non-Judging Self-Observer (a Key in the chapter on Keys), will allow you the opportunity to use these traits and skills in a more life-affirming way, or to change some of them. Just like water dissolved the Wicked Witch of the West, awareness erodes the all-powerful Jailer. How can this discovery, once realized, continue to be remembered, and then pave the way for a life-changing prison break? What could the implications of this discovery be?

If you read this short chapter under optimal conditions: a quiet room, no demands on your time, a focused mind, and physical comfort, you just might begin to notice that the Jailer's traits and skills are not unlike the material of the prisons. They are similar to the Prisons themselves. Sit back and as you read the resumes, decide which applicant would be best for the job. Which applicant would best keep *you* jailed?

These resumes are written in a humorous style (Ah but what truth doth lie in humor?).

Peter Fog

100 Repeat Lane, Programmedville, USA

E-mail: urbad@hotmail.com

JOB OBJECTIVE: Jailer

PERSONAL CHARACTERISTICS: Persistent, judgmental and highly critical. Specializing in self-sabotage.

EDUCATION: Home Schooled, Hometown, and World   Birth-Present

SPECIAL SKILLS: Fluent in Negative Self-Talk (any language); escape artist; specializing in diverse forms of anesthetization.

SUMMARY OF SKILLS:

Drama Archivist: collect, preserve, and vigilantly reinforce adaptations of original dramatic stories, horror stories, very grim tales, epics and historical fiction.

- Excellent Debater
- Perpetuator of guilt and shame
- Good attention to detail
- Comfort with repetition, comfort with repetition...
- Especially adept at using state of the art technology to play old tapes and make them sound like new.

WORK EXPERIENCE:

You Need To Pay, Inc., *Enforcer*

- Responsible for using emotional "trigger words' to help people constantly relive past guilt and shame
- Responsible for using motivational skills to instill a commitment to non-forgiveness.
- Responsible for subtle support of continued lack of self-esteem, subtle blockage of budding self-confidence, and subtle rebuttal of positive self-talk.

Play Them Again Sam, *Disc Jockey*   1983-1996

- Selection of appropriate tapes to impede personal development.
- Perfect timing; knows which tape to play when.
- Care and reinforcement of very old tapes to enable constant repetition of play.
- Attention to the slightest breakage (break-through) of old tapes to ensure repair for continued use.

Maria Cant

46 Narrow Lane, Smallview, Europe

E-mail: notenuf@optonline.net

PROFESSIONAL POSITION: Gediler

PERSONAL CHARACTERISTICS: Vigilant, Unrelenting, Focused, and Persuasive.

SPECIAL SKILLS: Ability to identify each individual's Achilles heel, stimulator of memories; defender of defenses; ability to work with large and diverse populations.

WORK EXPERIENCE:

They're Not Here, *Low-Bar Tender*   1944-1962

- Over serve patrons to assist forgetting.
- Listen and reinforce: it's not my fault, I can't do it: why me stories.
- Promote avoidance to ensure a breakthrough will not occur.
- Anesthetize, Anesthetize, Anesthetize.

Repetitive Behaviors, Inc., *Trainer*   1965-Present

- Teach techniques for reinforcement of negative patterns.
- Creative reenactment of original pain in a variety of life environments: work, personal relationships, and health related areas, with the focused goal of reinforcement.
- Strengthen irrational thinking and "stay in the box" thinking.
- Facilitate a masters class in the DANGERS of CHANGE; Emphasis on examples of the painful mistakes made by class members as they tried to make import-ant changes.
- Persuade trainees to practice the ancient behaviors to ensure their continuance into infinity.

EDUCATION:

School of Hard Knocks, World   Birth-Present

Princeton: MBA, Intranational Relations   1962-1965

SPECIAL AWARDS:

Unconscious Objector (all three years)

Superior memorization and recall of Ancient Tapes (all three years)

Kim Patterson

Overdo Drive, Asia

E-Mail: 1 more x@hotmail.com

JOB OBJECTIVE: Jailer

SPECIAL SKILLS:

Master of repetition, Master of repetition, Master of repetition:

Ability to endure stagnation for long periods of time.

Ability to trigger especially hurtful memories.

Energetic in stifling changes, positive movement.

Mender of breaks in the Protective Fort of childhood.

PERSONAL CHARACTERISTICS;

Inflexible

Associative Memory

Attention to minor detail

WORK EXPERIENCE:

Vintage Wear, *Pattern maker/teacher*   2000-Present

- Identified pattern to be cut out for each student.
- Had students replicate pattern to exact specifications.
- Specialized in preservation of patterns to pass on to student's future children.

Familiar Designs, Inc., *Owner/Operator*   1994-2000

- Developed successful business specializing in exact replication of historic designs.
- Taught the ancient art of weaving old threads into new material.
- Trained and supervised staff of fifty-six to create exact replicas of this new material.

EDUCATION:

Family Institute of Replicated Design   1970-1992

Family Institute of Replicated Design   1993-1994

Jason Wall

Childhood Downunder, Australia

E-Mail: Ihurt@core.set

JOB OBJECTIVE: Jailer

SKILLS SUMMARY; Worked as a mason for over 40 years. Handled the needs of a diverse population of clients in the repair of crumbling defense walls. Developed specialized mortar for maturing walls. Ability to listen and assess where client's walls might be vulnerable to breakthroughs endangering their future protection.

WORK EXPERIENCE

Sandcastles/Fortresses, Inc., *Designer*   2004-Present

- Design kits to assist children in early skills of protection through castle/fortress sand structures.
- Discovered coating to keep environment from destroying the fortress.
- Created exercises to encourage children to build and design their own fortress and supplied additional materials in each kit. Lifetime guarantee.

Invisible Protection, Inc., *Owner*   1997-Present

- Created concept of invisible mortarless walls of protection.
- Developed sensory sensitive materials.
- Conducted classes on self-repair if ever necessary.
- Trained builders at an international symposium.
- Taught teachers in the elementary school the process of invisible wall building.

Walls R US, *Mason*   1987-1997

- Skilled in a variety of wall designs.
- Invented the most enduring materials for construction.
- Interviewed clients to determine forms of protection needed.
- Developed specialized mortar for occasional cracks in protective walls.

EDUCATION:

Miami Technical High School   1986

Apprentice Program: Apprenticed 6 years to Mortimer Finite, Master Builder of Milan.

*Wrote award-winning pamphlet: "What Can't Be Seen, Others Can't Break".

I.E.Magine

1 Ancestor Drive

Familia, B.C.

PERSONAL CHARACTERISTICS: Imaginative, creative negative thinker, keen observer of behavior, thorough, great memory, expert in assumption.

SPECIAL SKILL: Produce scripts that evoke immobilizing emotions.

WORK EXPERIENCE:

ABC Writers Guild, Story developer/screenwriter, strong feelings   1980-Present

- Master of "Trigger Words."
- Developed method of "confusion" by having the story told through equally powerful conflicting points of view.
- Wrote scripts so actors could easily adapt the story line to their character and invest 100% in the story, forgetting it is not their own.
- Supervised endless rehearsals until parts are ingrained.

Scare Flicks Studio, *Horror film scriptwriter*   1959-1979

- Develop plots that produce immobilizing fear.
- Create story lines that encourage the viewer to image their own worst possible fears.
- Write scripts that allow viewers to make up their own version of the story as the plot unfolds and to anticipate outcomes based upon their personal version.

SPECIAL AWARDS:

Constancy in Form: Having the ability to always create the same outcome in each of my many films.

Best Psychological Horror Film: Use of the psychological technique of desensitization so viewers lose awareness of the horror and accept it as normal.

EDUCATION:

New York University, NYC   1975-1979

Hugo First

Pleasantville, N.Y.

E-mail: l IM@your disposal.com

PERSONAL CHARACTERISTICS: Patient, accommodating, empathetic listener, responsible, dependable.

EDUCATION:

United Nations School of Diplomatic Studies, NYC, NY

Ph.D. Interpersonal Relations 1950

Dissertation: International accommodation.

PROFESSIONAL EXPERIENCE:

Foryou University, Bronx, NY   1951-2001

POSITION: Professor of Interpersonal Relations

- Taught five classes per semester while acting as advisor to ten doctoral students.
- Facilitated interscholastic conference on "Niceness" as a dominant personality trait.
- Headed a think tank on "How to create the desire to always put others first."
- Senior member of team who interviewed 1500 people over a three-year period, for a study focused on the barriers to saying no and the areas of the brain involved in this process.
- Met the requirements of publishing every two years of my tenure (Actually published every year so I was more highly regarded and liked by the administration.)

SABBATICAL TRAVEL/STUDIES:

Traveled with three other colleagues and followed their agendas, missing four of the five countries I desired to see. Collaborated on a paper whose topic they decided upon. Recorded all thoughts whenever any occurred, and compiled them in a logical order to facilitate their future writing.

PUBLICATIONS:

- Twenty-Three Behaviors that Ensure Eventual Invisibility.
- How to Say Yes When your Heart, Soul, and Gut Scream "No!"
- Mirror, Mirror on the Wall Make Me Liked by One and All (five years on the top ten Best Seller list)

Rosa Pinpointa

Eyema, Peru

E-mail: intheline@.tow

SKILLS SUMMARY: Fifteen years experience in the area of animal training. Trained a variety of animals for their roles in film using my specialized technique of exclusionary focus. Developed a process to preserve visual filters for repeated use by domestic animals. Produced and directed the award-winning documentary, *The effects of blinders on domesticated animals as a behavior modification technique*. Studies are being done to replicate the successful outcome of the use of animal blinders in behavior modification with a small group of middle school children.

PERSONAL CHARACTERISTICS: Proficient in "in-the-box thinking," determined, hyper- focused, tenacious, comfortable with repetition, serious and work-oriented.

EDUCATION:

National Institute of Animal Trainers

    Certificate Program, 2000
    Apprenticed to Mr. Marvel of the Small World Circus, 2002

WORK EXPERIENCE:

"Rosa-Colored" Blinder, *Consultant*   2000-Present

- Trains animal handlers to effectively use "Rosa-Colored" Blinders to teach strict obedience to a command.
- Creates a Blinder product of great durability that will last a lifetime.
- Oversees laboratory experimentation on the applicability of blinders to humans, with the goal of eliminating confusing options and alternative routes. Greatly reduces the discomfort of choice.

All-Star Pets, *Owner*   1996-2000

- Worked with dogs chosen for roles in film, to reject by the process of reward/punishment a variety of enticements identified as desirable to each individual dog so they learned to stay on only one path.
- Tested prototype of my "Rosa-Colored" blinders on the more curious and adventurous pets. Use of blinders ensured repetition of same path selection even when confronted with a minimum of eight divergent paths.

See It My Way, Owner *Perspective Trainer for Domestic Animals*   1989-1996
*Use of reward/ punishment to train dogs in singular focus. Developed high-pitched tapes for subliminal reinforcement of limited directional perspective. Worked well with all breeds.

Jailer Role

Put a check next to the Jailers you might be:

- **Peter Fog** _____

- **Maria Cant** _____

- **Kim Patterson** _____

- **Jason Wall** _____

- **I.E. Magine** _____

- **Hugo First** _____

- **Rosa Pinpointa** _____

Part IV

Key Holder Role

CHAPTER EIGHT

Master Keys

- **Non-Judging Self-Observer (NJSO) Key**
- **Self-Questioning Key**
- **Courage Key**
- **Healthy-Risk Key**

The previous chapters described three roles that you unconsciously play when you are Your Own Worst Enemy: the role of Prisoner, the role of Prison Builder, and the role of Jailer. To these three roles we now add a fourth, the role of Key Holder. In this role, you are finally conscious and therefore able to discover and to use the keys that fit the locks of your self-made prisons.

Like most people you are probably familiar with keys. You have one or more on a keychain and each key fits a particular lock. You are aware that you possess these keys, that they can be held in your hands and that they are tangible. The Keys found in the next four chapters are different. You are not aware you possess them; they are held in your mind, heart and spirit, and they are intangible. But there may not be only a single Key that fits the lock of your prison door. Some prison locks need a combination of Keys before they will open and you can break free. Coming to the "Aha!" of awareness, the clarity of understanding, and the peacefulness of acceptance about the four roles you play do not necessarily lead to change. Using the Keys will lead to change and to freedom from your self-imposed prisons. As you read the description of each Key and decide if it will fit your prison's lock, let the following suggestions be a guide:

1) **Read about each Key. Get a feeling of whether or not you would even consider using this key in the lock of your prison.**

2) **Perhaps modify it to your style of operation so it would create a more valuable fit.**

3) **Close your eyes and picture yourself using the Key. How does it feel? What other ideas does it trigger? What dialogues can you image?**

4) **Consider doing some exercises suggested for the Key and see if they could be applied to your prison break.**

5) **Practice one step at a time. Start with the easier changes first.**

6) **Evaluate how it works, and then, if the Key fits, use it!**

The chapters in this Key Holder section contain descriptions of sixteen Keys, to help you, the Key Holder, find the ones available to you for your prison break. Take your time, take in the information given for each Key and review the six suggestions. If the Key can be of value to you, put it on your chain and use it.

The four Keys described in this chapter are the Master Keys. Once they are on your keychain, they open a path to the remaining twelve Keys. Change is not possible without awareness, but awareness is avoided if it is too painful. The first Master Key, *Non-Judging Self-Observer* (NJSO), is the Key to a less painful self-observance, one that leads to self-awareness. The second Key, *Self-Questioning*, is a stress-reducing Key. When using it there is no pressure to know the answers; it only assists in asking honest questions. Ironically, when the pressure of having to know is off, the answers to your questions will follow. The third Key is the *Courage Key*, which is hard to recognize, yet is found on every keychain. This is a Key you may be unaware you possess. It is held in your hands when getting out of bed, despite the pull of depression to stay under the covers, when facing an unhealthy workplace, or when feeling the pains in your body, mind and spirit. It takes the assistance of the *Courage Key*, to allow you even in the presence of fear, to try the other Keys that are needed to free you from your prisons. The fourth, and last, of the Master Keys is the *Healthy-Risk Key*. In order to become **Your Own Worst Enemy…No More**, change is necessary. Change and risk are inseparable partners, so risk is also necessary. For the description of the fourth Key, the *Healthy-Risk Key*, I will use a short illustrative story to explain the criteria for taking a healthy risk.

NON-JUDGING SELF-OBSERVER KEY (NJSO)

It's hard to change something you are not aware needs changing. It's hard to be aware when you are afraid to see yourself. It's hard to see yourself when you look through judgmental eyes.

Becoming an NJSO is the first Key to many prison doors. In some philosophies, this Self-Observer is called the Witness, Mindfulness, or Presence. Whatever the language, the act is freeing. If you know you won't be judged, you can courageously see things. Then you might be able to observe yourself and say, "I keep saying yes when I really want to say no. I have little time to do what I want or need. I feel so disorganized. I've been like this for a long time. Interestingly, I always need to please others." This self-observation did not include the hurtful name-calling that damages self-esteem and makes you afraid to look at yourself in the first place. Now that you see your behavior, without judgment, you can decide what you need to do differently.

Perhaps you have been forgetful lately. You didn't remember your dental appointment even though you had it written down on the calendar. You misplaced your glasses at least three times in one week and left your car keys on the counter where you made your last purchase.

Having done all this, you now carry on a litany of Negative Self-Talk. You say, "I'm losing my mind. This has to be early Alzheimer's. I can't remember anything; I'm a mess." With your *NJSO Key* in hand you free yourself from the prison of judging self-talk. You are able to step back and say, "I notice I'm very forgetful this week. It is such a busy week and I have a lot on my mind. This upsetting forgetfulness happens when I'm overloaded. I don't allow myself time to get rebalanced. I even observe myself holding my breath. How can I remember my appointments, glasses and keys when I don't even remember to breathe?" The **Non-Judging Self-Observer**, by not being judgmental, gives you an opportunity to see more clearly.

Let's say you have just gotten out of your third bad relationship. You start to make damaging self-judgments. You decide you are a loser, unlovable, and you can't ever have a successful relationship. Remembering to put the *NJSO Key* into action you now say, "This is the third relationship that has not worked out. I think I keep choosing people who can't possibly make a commitment. When I think about it, there were signs early on that Bob, Mike, and Bill didn't want a long-term relationship.

To use this Key you need to eliminate the killer self-talk, just step back, and be an observer. This moment of stepping back to observe yourself allows you to see, without judgment, what you might have seen before but could not afford to acknowledge. With *gentle* observation, you begin to know the right questions to ask yourself in order to put change into action.

The **NJSO** is your best friend. It is the part of yourself that knows you're okay. and that you're doing your best at any given moment. It is a Key that unlocks multiple prisons. Give it a turn!

SELF-QUESTIONING KEY

Never ask a question you don't want the answer to.[13] This advice implies that a question has to lead to an answer. The great value of the *Self-Questioning Key* is that you don't have to know the answer, and therefore can feel free to ask questions.

If you have the *NJSO Key* on your keychain, and add the *Self-Questioning Key*, you have a dynamic duo available to you. Once you learn the skill of observing yourself without painful judgment, you start to see your reality. Questions based upon reality eventually produce real answers, not answers someone else gives you or answers you wish were true. Real answers are based on what you have clearly observed. Freedom is having the courage to see reality, to ask yourself insightful questions, and to have the patience to let the answers evolve.

Let's say you have been trying to lose weight for the last ten years. You've been on over twenty different diets, some several times, and you either don't lose weight or don't keep the weight off. It is obvious to you that your weight is a prison you haven't been able to escape from. Now you're willing to try the keys of **NJSO** and **Self-Questioning** to unlock the prison door.

* * *

The following example looks in upon Yvonne, as she applies the *NJSO* and *Self-Questioning Keys* to her *Prison of Overweight*. Yvonne says to herself, "I see this last diet that I was on had no better results then the twenty others I tried. I know I am very responsible and disciplined in other areas of my life. I seem to be unable to apply this to dieting. I observe that I'm unable to stick to a diet, or I stick to it only until I lose weight and then slowly put the weight back on."

123

Using the *NJSO Key*, Yvonne is allowed to bring a neutral eye to the situation and actually see the reality of it. Now, she can add the **Self-Questioning Key**, knowing the questions are even more important than the answers. Yvonne asks herself the following questions:

1) **Why, when I'm so able in other areas, can't I lose the weight I want to lose?**

2) **Am I the one who wants to lose weight or is it really someone else's goal for me?**

3) **What could I possibly gain (secondary gain, an unconscious benefit) from keeping the the weight on.**

4) **Are there ways to lose weight that work better for who I am and how I reach a goal? Could the idea of a diet and focus on food not be good for me?**

5) **What might I be afraid of if I actually lose the weight?**

6) **Can I accept myself and have a good life at my present weight?**

These are just a few questions that can arise when you approach the observed reality with a gentle curiosity and not with the anxiety of needing immediate "right" answers. In this more relaxed approach, you might generate a question that you never before thought of or allowed yourself to ask. That previously unasked question could be the Key that will unlock your prison door and open you to a powerful freedom. In this example, Yvonne asks herself questions, and without forcing the answers, they lead her to a new way of approaching a problem she has wrestled with for many years. Questions are the Key! Try this short exercise of simply asking questions. (No answers required!)

1) Ask yourself two questions about some area in which you are stuck.

2) Ask yourself something you presently do not know the answer to.

3) Ask yourself one question each day.

The practice of asking yourself questions without the stress and fear of needing an answer is a gift of freedom. It is a freedom to unleash your mind and get to know yourself without judgment and stressful expectations.

COURAGE KEY

The *Courage Key* allows you to take in the reality seen by the **NJSO Key**. It is on the same keychain. They are powerful together. While the **NJSO** allows you to see reality and leads to **Self-Questioning**, the *Courage Key* opens the door to understanding what is seen. It further allows you to consider what, if anything, needs to be done with the reality. The **Courage *Key*** might be the key that frees you to take the risk of leaving a job that had a toxic environment, or a relationship that hasn't worked for many years. You might now be free to go back to school, or go on an African Safari. This key has many teeth and can take years to use with ease.

The *Courage Key* is not necessarily the courage we might think of when we think of heroes and heroines. The *Courage Key* can be the courage it takes to "just" get out of bed some days, or the courage to see the truth in any given moment so we can take action on that truth when it is necessary for our well-being. The *Courage Key* can be the courage to say no and to free yourself from the prison you are locked in where you can only say yes. When you have the courage to say no you teach people that you have the right to decide how to use your precious time.

The *Courage Key* is the companion to many of the Keys that free us from our prisons. When we calm ourselves with the *NJSO Key,* we might be aware, like the lion in the Wizard of Oz, that deep within ourselves is the courage we need to be free. Testing that courage in small and less risky ways validates its existence and allows us to experience little successes. Each small success can be built upon, creating a foundation to support your leap to freedom.

* * *

Mike makes use of three Master Keys: *NJSO*, *Self-Questioning*, and his recently acquired *Courage Key*. Mike says to himself, "I know I have changed jobs four times in the last two years. I worked so hard to become a CPA. Since I was little I was told I was a genius with numbers. I could always do the job well. I don't mind working, but after just a few months to half a year, I realize I don't want to go to work in the morning. The days drag and I can't sit still. I can't talk myself into sticking it out, even though I know I need to earn money. My wife Joan will be very upset. I'm not a quitter but I've already quit other jobs." Mike using the **NJSO Key,** is observing his reality without judging. The old, keyless Mike would use judging language. "I'm unstable. Something is really wrong with me. No one would ever choose to be with me. I'm lazy." But with his newly found Keys Mike can observe the facts of his present reality. Now Mike is free to use the *Self-Questioning Key* without needing immediate answers. He asks himself:

1) **Should I force myself to stick it out? Am I really lazy?**

2) **What didn't I like about my last four jobs?**

3) **Did I want to be a CPA or did someone else guide me in that direction?**

4) **What else could I now be?**

5) **Could Joan tolerate my career change?**

6) **Who could I talk to about this?**

Mike asks himself important questions. He might or might not know the answers at this moment, but having the courage (*Courage Key*) to ask opens up the prison doors and allows answers to follow.

For Mike, the *Courage Key* moves to the forefront, not with bells and whistles, but quietly. The *NJSO* and the *Self-Questioning*

Keys opens the way for questions to be asked in the first place, therefore creating an opportunity for courageous self-understanding (*Courage Key*). The questions Mike asks, when thought over, suggest that his present field of work is not right for him. He might be able to take his skills and transfer them to a career that is more suitable to his entire personality. Maybe he needs more mobility than an office job offers. Maybe his family's guidance, which made sense considering his natural abilities, didn't encourage him to explore what he would also enjoy. Maybe he isn't lazy, or a person who can't stick with anything. Maybe he is not a quitter, but a person in a career that doesn't fit who he is. Mike is starting to have the courage to see that a change could be necessary. The courage to see, ask, and understand can be frightening. Remember, *Courage is not the absence of fear but taking action in the presence of fear.*[14] To make a change, we need to take some risks. Enter the next Key, the *Healthy-Risk Key*.

HEALTHY-RISK KEY

Risk and change are Siamese twins. One can't happen without the other, even if the change only requires minimal risk. Change, and how people change, has long been a topic of interest in psychological circles. For example, Freud, the father of psychoanalysis, felt that the analyst's interpretations were a vital component, without which change wouldn't occur. Awareness and understanding were not enough. Karen Horney, a renowned psychoanalyst, believed that awareness and understanding alone did not produce change.

The belief of renowned professionals, and the experience of many, has shown that awareness and understanding (the longed for "aha!") do not automatically bring about change. What does? Using this new Key, the *Healthy-Risk Key*. The Keys already on this keychain are: the *NJSO Key*, the *Self-Questioning Key*, and the *Courage Key*. These can prepare you to take a risk in the form of action—a healthy risk, which, in turn, can set you free.

Before using this Key you may ask yourself, "What is a healthy risk? How do I know if I should take one? What's the downside of taking it? How can I take it if I'm so afraid?" See, you are already asking questions!

A healthy risk is not the same for everyone. What is a risk for me might be joyous for you. What might be a risk for you might be less frightening to me, and therefore less risky. That being said, a healthy risk will have common elements. Ask yourself:

1) **Have I decided this risk is finally necessary to take?**

2) **Will not taking it keep me in a place I can no longer stay?**

3) **Is taking the risk less dangerous, mentally, physically and spiritually, than not taking it?**

4) **Can I create optimal circumstances in which to use the Healthy-Risk Key?**

5) **Have I considered possible worst-case scenarios, which I need to consider before the Key is put in the lock?**

The answer is yes to all five questions. You have assessed the risk and know it is a healthy risk for you. Now, the important question is, "How do I take that risk? What do I do first?"

Take a breath and feel the comforting weight of the Keys in your pocket, then clearly state the healthy risk you have decided to take. Be clear! Write it out, or record it and listen. Remember, you decided it was more dangerous not to take this risk. Remember, you decided that even if the worst imagined outcome occurs, you still need to take this risk. Remember, you will take this risk in optimal circumstances. Optimal circumstances include a location in which you feel most safe, have a support system in place, and any additional information needed before you take action.

To make a start, break the risk into doable steps. Start with a step that feels less risky. Listen to your senses as well as your mind. If you are still hesitant, take a small risk in another non-threatening area that has a great chance of success, like walking home a slightly different way or ordering something different in a restaurant you are familiar with. These gentle risks allow you to experience success and to build upon your successes. This might sound silly, but it has merit. Success breeds success. Okay, back to your "risky risk".

Now you have decided upon the five steps needed in your risk-taking plan. You have ascertained that making an informational call is the least threatening. If a friend is there while you make the call, you believe you can do it. After the call, pick the second least-threatening step and see what help, if any, you need to complete this step. The following example can contribute to a better understanding and even be a map to follow in using the **Healthy-Risk Key** for your personal risk.

* * *

Paula has been home raising children for twelve years and is now ready to go back to school to get a degree in art history, her passion. She has hopes of either teaching or being connected to an art museum in some capacity. Paula is cognitively ready, but on an emotional level, she is petrified and finds she's immobile. She knows what she wants, she knows what she needs to do for it to happen, but she can't do it.

Paula, finding a book on healthy risk-taking, checks to see if the risk of going back to school meets the criterion of a healthy risk. She asks and answers the following:

1. Is this a risk "I" have decided is finally necessary to take?

Is going back to school a risk Paula (not her husband, children, or good friends) has decided to take? Paula checks yes to number one. She always told herself she wanted to be home until the children were in school full-time. Her husband's income afforded her the opportunity to fulfill this desire. Paula has loved art history since the sixth grade, when she had a teacher who was passionate in her teaching of Renaissance Art. Paula is letting her dreams and genuine inclinations have a voice.

If we observe, Paula is making use of the **NJSO Key** as she reviews her past thoughts and action. She is using the key of **Self-Questioning** and the **Courage Key** when she has the courage to honestly ask herself the questions needed to determine whether she is embarking upon a healthy risk. She happens to have the answers at this point in her evolution, but remember, the questions are more important than the answers. With the courage to know her truth, the answers usually follow.

2. Do I know and feel that not taking this risk will keep me in a place I can no longer stay?

Paula checks a shaky yes to number two. Paula has enjoyed being a stay-at-home mom with all its ups and downs, but in the last three years she has become restless and a bit depressed. An unsettling longing has been growing inside her—she wants to have her own time and to see herself more as an individual, rather than a mother or wife. Paula needs to add other aspects to her life right now.

3. Have I have decided taking the risk is less dangerous than not taking it?

Paula is unsure of her answer, because she is so immobilized. It seems to her that the risk of going back to school is great. On the other hand, she is starting to believe that if she doesn't try now, she will begin to feel dangerously worse. Paula puts a tentative check next to yes for question three. Paula is forcing herself to answer yes or no, when perhaps she needs to let the question stand unanswered a while longer and keep asking herself other questions. Maybe she needs to bring her senses in to facilitate knowing. She could visualize the choices and get a sense of how each feels, or sit in silence and attend to what comes to her in the grace of silence. Paula might have to ask herself this question again before deciding if it's a healthy risk.

4. Can I create optimal circumstances in which to take the Healthy Risk: safe location, support in place, additional information, if needed?

Paula can start by making a call from her home or looking on the Internet for schools in reasonable proximity to her home, that offer a degree in art history. Her home is a safe and comfortable environment in which to take her first real step. She might decide she needs the presence and support of a good friend while she makes the call, or someone who agrees to be available to talk to her right after the call. Paula is taking responsibility to create optimal circumstances so that her first step is successful. This will give her courage to take the second step.

5. Am I aware of possible worst-case scenarios, which need to be considered?

If Paula goes back to school, her household might become so disrupted that she can't handle anything. Her children might start having major problems, and her own mother could tell her she's a terrible mother. Her husband might feel neglected and talk about divorce. She could realize she's not smart enough or that she's too old to do the required schoolwork. She might even hate art history!

Now that she's looked at the worst of the worst-case scenarios, she has to see if the risk is worth it. She knows this level of catastrophe wouldn't be worth it, but realizes, as she's writing the above scenario, that it wouldn't reach that level. She would start out part-time to see how school fit into her schedule, where the holes were that she needed help with. Her husband would be somewhat supportive because he will only benefit by Paula being happier. She has already talked to him about possible effects on the family's routines if she pursues school. Her mother worked, so she'd have some understanding. Paula has loved art history for many years, so why would she hate it now? The real worst case scenario-disruption of routines; the children's upset over change; her husband's adjustment to change, her mother's partial understanding; and her own dislike of some of the course work-is an acceptable risk.

Paula's risk has four of the five common elements of a healthy risk. The third element (taking the risk is less dangerous than not taking it) only generated a shaky yes. Maybe she is not ready to take the action required by a healthy risk. Perhaps she needs more information, more supports in place, more discussions with her family, or more self-questioning before she uses the *Healthy-Risk Key*.

Three months later, Paula is able to give a clear yes to the third element. She decides that taking the risk is less dangerous than not taking it and she enrolls in a degree program for art history.

Master Keys

Put a check(s) next to the keys you feel you need:

- **Non-Judging Self-Observer (NJSO) Key** _____
- **Self-Questioning Key** _____
- **Courage Key** _____
- **Healthy-Risk Key** _____

CHAPTER NINE

The Mind-Shift Keys

- The Patience key
- The Change-of-Perspective Key
- The Success-in-Trying Key
- The Think-Out-of-the-Box Key

You can't have too many Keys. Your Own Worst Enemy shudders when it hears the rattle of the Keys on your keychain. In this chapter, we add four more Keys for you to try out. These Keys are the Mind-Shift Keys.

They unlock barriers that have kept you imprisoned; barriers caused by limited thinking. The Mind-Shift Keys open you to a variety of new choices needed for your prison break. To be Your

Own Worst Enemy...No More you need to make conscious changes. Change is a shift from what was. The process of change takes time and practice and is sometimes uncomfortable. With the **Patience Key** in hand, you are able to tolerate the discomforts of this process. The **Change-of-Perspective Key** allows you to see how even a small shift in your thinking can make a world of difference. For example, a prisoner who, attempted, for twenty years to escape through the small window in his cell. In his hundredth attempt he pulled at the window bars yet again, fell off his cot, and in tumbling back toward the prison door, noticed it was open. It had always been open!

Once you have the patience to see things differently and change your limited perspective, you might start reassessing some of the imprisoning stories you have told yourself throughout your life. One of those stories might be that success is only possible if the desired outcome is met. Anything short of that outcome is failure. Failure is painful and might damage your self-esteem. With the **Success-in-Trying Key** firmly in hand, you might then make a shift in your criteria for success, and see that the act of trying is successful in itself! What unlimited possibilities await, if you have the courage to try. It is easier to try if that trying is viewed as success. The last Key in this Mind-Shift chapter is one that unlocks brain cells that might never have been used, and therefore were never available for your conscious prison break. It's a playful Key with seriously positive results: the **Think-Out-of-the-Box Key**.

PATIENCE KEY

Is developing patience easier said than done? Yes. Is it worth a try? Yes. Change can take more time than we are comfortable with. It took time to have the courage (*Courage Key*) to be conscious of your situation and even more time to see it without painful and often immobilizing judgment (*NJSO Key*). Then you asked honest questions of yourself (*Self-Questioning Key*) that allowed you to make a plan and to analyze the level of risk (**Healthy-Risk Key**). All of these Keys precede a healthy action and pave the way to a successful prison break. Most prison breaks are a multi-Key job! The Key that accompanies the previous four Keys and that will be present while you take your first baby steps, or giant leap of faith is the *Patience Key.*

A reacquaintance with patience might be necessary before you are willing to accept this Key's help. From an early age, you might have been told to be patient when it was truly impossible for you to even understand that concept. To a child, an hour seems like a day and a day like a week. You might still have residual feelings of frustration when patience is called for, triggered back to the time when you really didn't have the cognitive ability to befriend patience. Time is relative for all of us, and the same twenty-four hours that speed by when life is good go painfully slowly when life is bad.

There are many sayings about what comes to "him who waits," but not about how to handle the discomfort of the wait. If it's so uncomfortable, why put effort into developing patience? What is the value of the *Patience Key*? What is patience anyway? Patience is intangible; it is a state of being. When you consciously choose it, it is felt and seen by you and all around you. It touches everyone. Patience is a seed to be cultivated. When it blooms, it frees you from your impatience with life's many frustrations. It frees you from your impatience with yourself caused by unreasonable expectations.

Expectations can be a prison. Who said you should be anywhere else than where you are right now? But, you say to yourself:

"I'm thirty/forty/fifty/sixty and I only earn (X) I should earn (Y)."

"I'm thirty/forty/fifty/sixty and I was just laid off. I'm not employed."

"I'm (X) years old and I'm not in a relationship. I've never been married."

"I'm still in a terrible marriage. I should have gotten out fifteen/ten/five/two, years ago. I'm thirty+ and I still don't have children."

"I don't own a house. I just lost my house. I'm thirty/forty/fifty/sixty/seventy years old and I own nothing."

These are not imagined experiences; they are painfully real. The goals you set and the expectations you had, in many cases, were realistic and you were willing to work to reach those goals and fulfill those expectations. They just didn't happen, or they happened and then, shockingly, all the work you did got undone. The present reality is not what you had expected. It is not what you worked towards. It's not how you wanted it to be.

How can anyone be patient and use the *Patience Key* in these situations? You can learn to be patient in these situations by making conscious choices over and over and over again; choices about your reactions and about your self-talk in response to these situations. You can use the *Patience Key* to unlock the prisons that impatience builds.

You have hundreds of opportunities each day to practice patience. Many situations are not as earthshaking as the situations just mentioned, but they provoke of a host of emotions that can imprison you. In all the following situations, you have the choice to be patient, but not right away. Patience takes practice.

You're on a tight schedule and you're sitting at the third red light in a row.

You make a call to correct a mistake on a bill and you are listening for the twelfth go-around to somebody's version of "waiting" music.

You are at the checkout at the supermarket and just when it's your turn, the cashiers are switching drawers.

When we have an emotional reaction to the frustrations we face, our brain chemistry has a field day of emotions for ninety seconds. For those ninety seconds your choices are limited. In the ninety-first second, it is back in your lap. You now have many choices, but let's look at three. You can consciously choose: to avoid a situation; to alter a situation; or to accept a situation. The **Patience Key** is needed for the last two.

What are the steps that allow use of the **Patience Key**?

Step 1. PTP (Patience Takes Practice). Say this three-word phrase to yourself throughout your brain's ninety-second chemical reaction. Say it each time patience is one of your response choices.

Step 2. Stay present and stay aware of the situation and of your reactions to it. Use the help of the **NJSO** and **Courage Keys.**

Step 3. Decide either to alter or to accept the situation when avoiding is not possible. Use the **Self-Questioning Key** and the **Healthy-Risk Key.**

Step 4. Breathe, exhale, and tell yourself to relax.

Step 5. Healthy self-talk is a critical step for patience to prevail.

Step 6.   Practice, practice, practice. Mess up and then practice, practice, and practice again.

Let's use a short story to better illustrate the six steps it takes to develop patience. We will present a situation where Molly decides to alter a situation.

Story

Molly is beginning to feel the old familiar dread creeping up on her as the annual family cruise is approaching. This tradition was started four years ago by Molly's mother and her siblings to take all their children and grandchildren for a week's cruise as a way to keep the geographically distant families connected. In theory, this is a thoughtful gesture; in reality, it gives no thought to the oil-and-water personalities of several family members.

Molly works very hard and doesn't have the time for a vacation; going on the cruise causes her more stress than her work. Her Uncle Ralph, her mother's oldest brother, is nasty when he drinks, which he does at every lunch and dinner. He says things that embarrass her mother, but no one says a thing because he is the pseudo-patriarch of the family. Molly has promised herself that this time she is going to find a way to not let Uncle Ralph spoil the vacation.

Step 1. *PTP (Patience Takes Practice).*

Remembering the last four cruises, Molly knows that as soon as her Uncle Ralph says something to embarrass her mother, Molly snaps at him and embarrasses her mother even more. She now knows it takes ninety seconds for her chemistry to have its day, so she decides on this cruise to alternate saying PTP over and over again, along with taking conscious deep breaths during her ninety second chemical reaction. She can practice patience by doing this first step each time Ralph enrages her.

Step2. *Stay Present and Aware. (Use **NJSO** and **Courage Keys**.)*

Molly is willing to observe, without judgment, her physical, emotional, and cognitive reactions to Uncle Ralph. She has the courage to ask her husband for a funny, agreed-upon signal to help in this awareness. This practiced awareness gives Molly a chance to do her part differently.

Step 3. *Decide! Alter or accept when avoiding is not an option. (Use **Self-Questioning** and **Healthy-Risk Keys**.)*

When Molly decides she isn't willing to miss the cruise as a way to avoid Uncle Ralph's behavior, she has to decide to either alter or accept the situation that makes her dread the cruise. She first asks herself what she can alter. Having courage to see the reality, she realizes she cannot stop Uncle Ralph from drinking; the fact that alcohol is available for passengers at lunch and dinner is out of her control. She can control are her reaction or her presence at some of the meals.

Another thought, which involves greater risk, is talking to her uncle in private. The risk of talking to her uncle while on the cruise, she decides, is too great. His reaction could possibly spoil the whole experience for everyone. Molly decides a change in attitude is what she can alter.

Step 4. *Breathe, exhale, and tell yourself to relax.*

Molly writes step 3 on an index card as a reminder at each lunch and dinner.

Step 5. *Healthy self-talk.*

Before each meal Molly tells herself she will sit as far away from her uncle as possible and that she will give her mother a smile or hug before and after each meal at which Uncle Ralph embarrasses her. She tells herself that everybody knows to ignore Uncle Ralph. She comforts herself by telling herself that she will speak to him when they get home from the cruise.

Step 6. *Practice, practice, practice. Mess up and then practice, practice, and practice.*

Molly says the words "patience takes practice" many times when Uncle Ralph makes his remarks. She sits as far away as she can and out of earshot when possible. On the second night of the cruise, when Uncle Ralph has a few too many and is in rare form, Molly momentarily loses it and shouts at him, "Enough!" She is able to control her reactions the rest of the shared mealtimes.

Molly knows she is the one who has to do things differently if she is going to have a different experience on this cruise. She puts into practice the six steps that helped her remain patient in a situation that had sorely tested her patience in the past. The *Patience Key* frees her to enjoy her vacation.

* * *

You now have the *Patience Key* available to you. Practice, practice, and practice. The **Patience Key** is an important addition to your keychain.

CHANGE-OF-PERSPECTIVE KEY

This next Key is the one needed to facilitate the use of the Keys that will follow. To change your perspective, you first need to know the meaning of the word perspective as it is being used here. Put simply, perspective is how you see things and what you tell yourself about what you see; your "take" on something; your point of view.

Your perspective is built upon and colored by all of your experiences: your enculturation, your schooling, and your personality (both nature and nurture). Your perspective has strong stuff behind it. It accompanies you everywhere, and over time you develop a belief that your perspective is the right one. The unconscious setting-in-stone of one's perspective becomes a prison. Have you ever said, or just thought, "If only she could see it differently"? Or "If only he could feel differently"? Have you ever wished you could see or feel differently? Feeling differently is a direct result of seeing differently—it's having a change of perspective.

In a workshop on creative thinking, I gave the participants an exercise to get up and change seats. Not a Herculean task, but it was very uncomfortable. By the third session the participant's self-assigned seat had become a comfort zone. We are unconsciously drawn to and find comfort in the familiar. Each week they automatically took the seat they chose at the first class. So what's the point of the exercise? To get another point of view.

In the new seat, each person could see something he or she had not seen when sitting in the old seat. A simple change opened up another way of seeing. It made an immediate impact, and in the remaining three sessions the participants consciously started taking different seats and commenting on the new things they could now notice.

How can you transfer this "aha!" experience from a classroom into your life? How can you learn to change such an unconscious and ingrained part of yourself? By using the support of the other Keys already on your chain:

- By applying the *NJSO Key*, you can safely observe how your present perspective, in a problematic situation, might imprison you and keep you from a healthy outcome.

- The *Courage Key* will let you own the part your present perspective plays in the problem.

- The *Self-Questioning Key* stimulates broader seeing by letting you ask yourself, "How do I see this?" "How is the way I see this contributing to the problem?" "How else can I see this, and how else, and how else? "Am I willing?" "What am I not seeing?"

- The *Healthy-Risk Key* will allow you to assess if the risk of changing your perspective is a healthy risk to take.

- The *Patience Key* lets you take the time you need to make the changes you choose.

Because romantic partners often come from different family cultures, different life experiences, and in heterosexual relationships, different genders, there's a good chance they will see several things differently. These differences in perspective can sometimes be the cause of relationship problems.

Story

Eva and George have been living together for five years. They have just had yet another fight about money, some really nasty things have been said, and they have not spoken for two days. Their fights around the handling of money have escalated and Eva is worried it could do fatal damage to their relationship.

Eva is about to use the *Change-of-Perspective Key*, as well as the other Keys, to resolve the latest serious fight she and George had over money and to change this dangerous "dance" they do. In her kitchen, calming herself with tea, she is able to use the *NJSO Key*. She sees how her present perspective (that it is okay to have debt, and to put a trip on a credit card and pay it off over several months) gets George crazy. George's mother used credit cards irresponsibly and got the family into serious debt. Inflexibly holding on to her perspective puts her and George in the Prison of Unhealthy Patterns, and the Prison of "Rigidity."

The *Courage Key* lets her own her part in their problem—her unwillingness to budget and have the money in hand before booking a trip. The Self-Questioning Key lets Eva ask herself, "Why do I need to do it this way? How can I do my part differently?" She realizes it's just force of habit. That's the way she's always done it. She's not uncomfortable with reasonable debt, and she really really doesn't budget well. How else can she do it? She can ask George for help with a budget, or maybe someone else who could be more patient with her lack of skill in this area. Talk with George. Write him a letter or e-mail, letting him know she understands where his concern comes from, but she'd like him to remember that she has never gotten their family into trouble with her approach. Maybe they can compromise. One way to do it differently is sometimes they can save the money first and sometimes put it on credit, when they know they can pay it off in no more than three months.

She asks herself if she is willing to see it another way, to compromise. Eva's answer is yes. She really loves George; this is their only area of serious contention. The steps of the *Healthy-Risk Key* will help Eva put this modified perspective into action, and the *Patience Key* will help her through the fear and frustration of approaching money matters differently. Will it work? Who knows? The trying alone is the change of perspective that opens prison doors.

The mind shift that occurs, when you have a change in perspective, is an openness to new avenues of thought. One new avenue it can lead you to is the "joy of trying." This segues into our next Key, the *Success-in-Trying Key.*

SUCCESS-IN-TRYING KEY

You really need to be clutching your *Change-of-Perspective Key* when learning to use this next Key, the *Success-in-Trying Key*. The *Change-of-Perspective Key* can free you from being locked in the Prison of Rigidity with all the prisoners who believe in the philosophy of "all or nothing," "black or white." To these prisoners who never see success in trying, success will always rely on reaching the hoped-for outcome,. With this mindset, these prisoners close the door on trying because not reaching the outcome is too frightening. They would see themselves as failures.

When you are willing to make a change, it can be frightening. There are so many unknowns out there, so many possibilities for failure, so much vulnerability. How can you make change easier on yourself? How can you soften the experience as you swim in unknown waters?

You can do this by using two Keys: first, the *Change-of-Perspective Key*. This Key allows you to consider the possibility that the act of trying—and not only the outcome—is a valid measure of pride and success. Now you are ready to use the second Key, the *Success-in-Trying Key*, to take action on your new perspective. Why would this key make change less frightening? How could it change your life for the better?

Perhaps you won't try something because you are afraid you will fail. You are afraid you will embarrass or humiliate yourself. You are afraid people will judge you to be incompetent, or stupid, or foolish. Fear appears in every sentence; the fear of an unsuccessful outcome imprisons you. But what if...you changed the criterion for success? Success would be in the trying. It would be in the courage to try something new, not in a successful outcome. This different perspective— success is in trying, not in the outcome—is a key to freedom. Truth be told, you have little control over any outcome. Too many other people and variables are involved.

If trying is the success, if trying itself is valid, there is no failure. There is nothing you can't try. You have given yourself the gift of opening up your world to the exploration available to a healthy, unhampered person. Life can profoundly change when living that altered perspective.

If this were easy you might have already made this change and swung open that prison door. But other people (societies, cultures, your own family) might strongly advocate that success is in outcome. "If you don't succeed at first, try, try again,"[15] is a well-known proverb. Persistence is valuable and is an important part of succeeding. But where is the proverb, "If you don't succeed at all, be proud that you tried"? It's right here!

What happens when you put value on trying, as well as on a successful outcome? You become less afraid, you become less stressed, and you become more adventurous, more curious, and more playful. De-emphasizing the outcome is a healthy guilt-reducer. That's what happened for me. Speaking with some friends about our parenting, someone said they think we can be responsible for the process, how we parent, but not the outcome. The more I thought about this, the more peace it gave me. It opened the door of my self-created parent prison, "It's all my fault," and it let me reconsider how I saw my parenting and what I saw as my value. I realized that I could only do the best I was capable of at the time. I could take responsibility for my parenting process (trying), but I was not responsible for the final outcome of that process.

Story

In our next vignette, Luis is asked to speak at a local Career Guidance Center. The center is a small organization and the staff knows each other's families. Marina is the office manager and she has asked her husband, Luis, to be one of the speakers on a panel of small business owners. Luis has never done public speaking. He doesn't want to disappoint Marina or the staff, but he is petrified of standing up in front of a group of people and giving a talk. He would rather do almost anything else.

He is afraid he will make a fool of himself. He is afraid the other speakers are more educated and will think he is stupid. He is afraid he will embarrass Marina. Luis is a man who has taken many risks. He came to America on his own and worked fourteen hours a day to save the money to buy equipment to start a lawn service business. His first attempt failed because he took on more than he could handle, but his present business is growing at a more manageable rate.

Marina has told Luis that the center is grateful that he is even considering being on the panel. He just needs to tell the small audience how he went about starting a business, and maybe the possible pitfalls. She said it might make them less afraid when they hear that his first attempt didn't work, but that he was proud he took the risk and tried.

Luis is still afraid, but he knows the steps he took to start his business and he thinks he can tell an audience his own story. He remembers how he felt when his first business attempt failed. A retired business owner helped Luis see the pride he could take in having been courageous enough to try to start a business. He helped Luis see he could learn by his mistakes, and that trying is the only way to get where you want to go. Luis tells Marina he will do it. He hopes he can get across to the audience, even if he doesn't say it so well, that trying is good. Trying is success. Maybe others will see that they can even make a speech if they have to, and that it will be okay if it isn't perfect. Luis, in taking this risk of trying, will reinforce his new mind shift: that trying, not only outcome, is success.

The **Success-in-Trying Key** has been added to Luis' keychain. By knowing the value of trying, he has optimized his options. Now he is free to try anything!

As Luis has discovered, being unafraid to try is freeing. With that one mind shift you can truly expand your world and unlock the door to new experiences, a door that fear of failure has barred you from.

The last Key in this chapter is the **Think-Out-Of-The-Box Key**. It enables you to optimize your options.

THINK-OUT-OF-THE-BOX KEY

Think-out-of-the-box? What box? I'm not in a box!

The box we're talking about has no visible sides, no bottom, and no top. It's more like the invisible fence that is used to train animals not to go beyond a certain perimeter. After two to three weeks the animal doesn't even try. The analogy is imperfect in an important way. The animal did not put up the original barrier and cannot remove it. You might not have created the original box that keeps you from going further, or leaving your comfort zone, but you now keep yourself in it. You even forget it exists.A box is something that keeps you from movement, from change; it keeps you from going in a direction you'd like to go. It's a prison. How can you think out of a box, you don't know you're in? You can't! The first step is becoming aware of being boxed in. This awareness comes in reverse order. What I mean is, you see what it's like to be out of the box and only then realize you were in the box. Confused? Here is a clarifying example. This vignette, unlike the other vignettes, which are fictitious, is a true story of an experience I had thirty years ago.

My Story

My story begins when my son comes home from his sixth-grade Thinking Skills course. He has a problem to solve and shows me a picture of nine dots—three rows of three dots—in a square box. The problem is to connect the dots without picking up your pen or going over any line. No problem, I say to myself, and decide to try it after I'm finished with my work. Fast forward and there I am at 2:00am, tired, frustrated, and unsuccessful. It took strength not to wake him up and make him show me the solution, which he had accomplished before he went to sleep.

In the morning I greeted him with, "Show me the way you connected the dots." Lo and behold, he had to go out of the box to do it. "No!" said I. "You can't go out of the box." But his teacher had only said not to lift your pen or go over a line, she hadn't said you couldn't go out of the box. Off he went to school, and I sat in my kitchen and had an "aha!" moment. I realized I wasn't able to think "out of the box" to solve that puzzle. When I had gone to school, we couldn't draw outside of the lines. We walked the halls in lines so straight that the military would be put to shame. After this experience with my son's assignment, I realized that solutions could lie out of the box. I also realized I was in a box.

One week later, I had an opportunity to put this lesson into action and make The **Think-Out-of-the-Box Key** mine forever. I was on a forty five-minute business flight to Buffalo, NY. We were ready to land and were told to put our trays back into position. My tray wouldn't go into position, though I tried numerous times. The announcement to return your tray to its position, made on every flight, always suggested to me that it would be a danger to the landing process if this command wasn't followed. The thought that I, the person with the tray down, would be the cause of the plane crashing allowed me to accept my seat partner's offer to try to put the errant tray into position.

I could relax now; he would be responsible for any crash. I was able to calmly watch him do exactly what I did, move the tab from left to right, and continue to do so even though it wasn't working. "Um," I said to him, "maybe you should move the tab from right to left." He did, the tray stayed up, and I reinforced what I had learned through my son's "attach the dots" problem the week before. If I got out of the box there was a solution available to me, a solution that I couldn't see when I was in the box. Twenty-five years later, I still get peace from that lesson. Many times I may not know the answer, but if I get out of the box I'm imprisoned in, there are previously unseen solutions available to me. Even though I don't know at that moment what those solutions are, I have peace in knowing that they're out there. Most boxes are packed tightly so there will be no movement. There isn't room for expansion of what is contained inside. If you're going to have more room for growth, you have to get out of the box. Remember the example of the prisoner who thought the only way out of his cell was through the window? One day he pulled so hard at the bars on the window that he fell backwards, and for the first time noticed that there was another way out. The door had been open the whole time. That prisoner was forced to change his perspective, but what if he had had the *Think-Out-of- the-Box Key* on his chain? It would have opened his mind from the beginning to all the possibilities of escape from his prison cell, and perhaps saved him years of unnecessary imprisonment.

How do you find out if you're in a box? Use some of the Keys already on your keychain.

- The *NJSO Key* will let you put a non-critical eye on the things that keep you from moving in the direction you want to go.
- Having the *Courage Key* around helps you see the truth.
- The *Self-Questioning Key* lets you ask yourself "What box could I be in? What ways haven't I thought of that could help me move forward? What can I try that I've never tried before? What am I not seeing?"

Thinking out of the box is a creative approach to problem solving. When it is coupled with the *Success-in-Trying Key* it frees you from the prison of boxes you have kept yourself in, and it opens new worlds. This Key allows you to expand your mind, to use those brain cells that are unavailable to you when you are engaged in limited thinking. Do it another way. Draw out of the lines, be playful, and unleash yourself.

What might your day look like if it was guided by out-of-the-box thinking? It might include a change as simple as wearing a color you told yourself was "not you," one that others would never expect to see you wear. What fun to see their expressions! If you are a woman, it might be the day you sign up for an auto mechanics course that you have wanted to take. You love cars and would love to know how to fix them. Women in your family "wouldn't do that," so your mind was not able see that course as a possibility. Your out-of-the-box thinking experiment would allow you to jump out of the family box and sign up. Or you might decide you are going to take that trip to Venice. Now you need to get out of the box you've been in that has kept you from believing a trip like this was ever possible. Stepping out of the box of "impossible," you're going to think of all the ways you can save money for the trip of your dreams.

For the most effective use of Chapter Nine, remember to apply the six suggestions from chapter Eight (see page 114). See if any of the *Mind-Shift Keys* will work for you. The *Mind-Shift Keys* are powerful. They show you how a small shift can make a world of difference. Once they are on your keychain, along with the *Master Keys*, you are ready for the next set of Keys: the *Potential-Expansion Keys* described in the next chapter.

Mind-Shift Keys

Put a check(s) next to the keys you feel you need:

- **The Patience key** _____

- The Change-of-Perspective Key _____

- The Success-in-Trying Key _____

- The Think-Out-of-the-Box Key _____

CHAPTER TEN

Potential-Expansion Keys

- The Optimize-Options Key
- The Embrace-the-Unknown Key
- The Self-Trust Key
- The Self-Esteem Key

Your Own Worst Enemy is weakened with each turn of a Key. The next four keys are the Potential-Expansion Keys, which stand on the shoulders of the previous eight. When using the **Optimize-Options Key**, a more expansive way of thinking becomes available to you, that will aid in the creation of more options. You can now engage in the process of building a stockpile of options to use for your prison break. The **Embrace-the-Unknown Key** is one of the scariest Keys to put on your keychain. When you are considering its use, the **Courage Key** is of great assistance. As scary as it is on the one hand, is how potentially expanding it is on the other.

In research for a Wisdom Workshop that a colleague and I created, we identified an important wisdom tool. This tool is the knowledge that it is wiser to learn how to become more comfortable with uncertainty, than to try to become more certain. Life is uncertain; it is unknown! When you are able to embrace the unknown, you can free yourself from the Prisons of Worry and Fear. These are barriers to living life fully. When you embrace the unknown, you stay in the present, where all opportunities can be found to fulfill your potential. The **Self-Trust Key** isn't easily acquired. It requires battles with old ingrained versions of yourself, and with Negative Self-Talk. Once the battles are won, the expansion of your potential knows no bounds. Self-trust unlocks doors never before opened. The **Self-Trust Key** is the Key to using the **Self-Esteem Key**. Once you learn you can trust yourself, you automatically have more self-respect. Two necessary components for a healthy relationship are mutual trust and respect. A healthy relationship with yourself increases your self-esteem. The **Self-Esteem Key** opens you to all you are and can still become. When finally on your keychain, it unlocks many prison doors.

OPTIMIZE-OPTIONS KEY

This Key is preceded by the *Think-Out-of-the-Box Key*. It can take several Keys to unlock a prison door. Many have complex locks! Once you have that key on your chain, you can effectively use the **Optimize-Options Key**. Having options is like having pieces of gold. It enriches your life. It does this in a multitude of ways and is a great stress reducer. When you no longer feel trapped by having only one way to do something, one answer to your own questions, one career path, and only one right person for you, your stress level plummets. Having options calms the disquiet of stress, replacing it with a peaceful feeling.

Having more options awakens you to more opportunity. When changing jobs, this Key allows you to recognize that there are other career paths that your present skills are transferable to. It encourages you to take action, and to believe that there are several jobs you qualify for and would find rewarding, besides the one you are leaving. Life is scary, but less so, if, when a familiar door closes, you are holding the *Optimize-Options Key*.

With this Key in your hand, you can enter a bank and ask for the different ways they can help you handle your debt, and find one that is most beneficial to your financial future. You may have a friend who got help working out a more flexible payment plan, and another who decided to declare bankruptcy, but maybe neither of those options seems right for your situation.

With the *Optimize-Options Key* (the opportunity maker) you are comfortable asking for other solutions. After exploring options, the two solutions that your friends have chosen might wind up being the only reasonable choices for your situation. What is freeing is that you were aware that you could seek other options. Consciousness of options leads to freedom.

Story

Tara wanted to organize a fundraiser for her neighbor. Their child was in need of an immediate heart transplant, but the cost not covered by their insurance was staggering. Tara hadn't done anything like this before and was not sure what activity would have the potential to raise the most funds.

She decided to get together with other neighbors who had expressed a desire to help. They could encourage each other to use out-of-the-box thinking as preparation for optimizing the fundraising options. They decided to see how many creative ways they could use the "heart" theme to attract donations. The heart, they all agreed, was a recognizable symbol of caring.

First Bea suggested having a heart-shaped cake bake sale. All agreed it was a good idea but would not raise enough money. They decided it could be part of the event. Sam, a professional musician, said a concert with groups he could get to volunteer for the event would attract a larger crowd. Playing off both Bea's and Sam's ideas Tara had another idea. The groups could play only songs that had "heart" in the title. Creative, but how could that bring in a lot of money? Tara smiled. A dance contest. People could sponsor the dance teams to be able to dance from five minutes to three hours. "Or even single dancers," someone shouted. The sponsors could donate from a quarter to a dollar a minute. A business could sponsor at even higher rates. The box was opening and the options were flowing.

Fahwad said they should have a theme song — something catchy they could ask the local radio station to play. That decided it. They would use Van Buren Benny's lyrics to the song "You've Gotta Have Heart."[16] Fahwad broke into song.

They were on a roll and decided to link together "miles and miles of hearts" that people could pin money and checks on. Reva would be in charge of periodically retrieving the funds and securing them in a metal box. Options were being optimized left and right. Tara felt supported and sure of success in their trying!

Tara also unwittingly used the next Key on our chain, the **Embrace-the-Unknown Key**, when she decided to do something she had never done before: organize a fund-raiser.

EMBRACE-THE-UNKNOWN KEY

The unknown is uncomfortable. Maybe terrifying would be a better word. Actually, the feelings connected to the unknown lie on a continuum from uncomfortable to terrifying. The unknown is all-present. Ben Franklin's statement, the adage that "In this world nothing can be said to be certain except death and taxes,"[17] speaks to the reality that almost everything is unknown.

In a workshop titled "Shattered Dreams & Growth," created and facilitated by Ken Moses Ph.D., he described the intangible unknown in a way that makes it knowable on a sensory level. In this workshop he addressed the feelings a person encounters during a difficult change. At times you have what he called "a crack in your universe." Picture yourself in an egg, which represents your present world; you suddenly notice a crack in the egg. "Uh oh," you say. It takes you years to get the courage to look through that crack, and then when you do, what do you see? The Big Unknown. You hear yourself say, "I don't think so," as you plaster over that crack in an egg you've outgrown.[18] When you are facing the unknown, you may feel afraid. You might feel stupid because you just don't know. You could feel embarrassed because of your not knowing, or you could feel the familiar "I'm not enough." Who would want to feel this way? Who wouldn't stay in the familiar egg and try to deny, anesthetize, or detach from these feelings? Very few. Perhaps only those who hold the *Embrace-the-Unknown Key*.

But why would you want a Key that can free you to go into an unknown abyss? Because that is where healthy growth occurs, and that is the soil of new, uncharted worlds. Galileo had this Key, Marco Polo had this Key, and Rosa Parks had this Key. This is a Key that frees us to move forward, maybe only two steps, maybe quaking and shaking, but forward movement nevertheless.

Other Keys on your chain can support you; they can help you to be less afraid to use this very powerful Key to freedom. Keys can be used individually, but when they are combined to fit your personal needs, the synergy is empowering. When using the *Self-Questioning Key*, the *Courage Key*, and *Healthy-Risk Key*, ask yourself, "What risk could I have the courage to take, if I had this new Key in my hand?" You may not have the answer just now. Remember, the questions will lead to answers. Maybe you already have an answer, or answers, to that question. Using the *Embrace-the-Unknown Key*, what would be the next step you'd take in order to escape the Prison of Fear of the Unknown?

Let's listen in as our characters dialogue with themselves, and observe what other Keys they use to get to the *Embrace-the-Unknown Key*.

Story

Misha asks herself, "If I had the *Embrace-the-Unknown Key* in my hand, could I have the courage to risk telling my partner that I feel we have become strangers over the last six months? I have never said anything, in our five years together, that expressed upset about the relationship. I have kept my uncomfortable feelings to myself. This openness would be uncharted territory. How will Jake react? What will be the effect on our relationship? Maybe I should spackle over the crack in the egg of my relationship. But if I take a step into that unknown, and say how I've been feeling, it could prevent an even bigger crack. I can even open the door to a new and better relationship. I'll give it a little more thought."

Let's listen in on the unknown that Sam is dealing with: the crack in the egg of his safe world. Sam thinks to himself, "If I had the *Embrace-the-Unknown Key* in hand, I might have the courage to take the risk of being alone, and maybe lonely, before I enter a new relationship." *Be alone.* When Sam says these words to himself, the dark and chilly unknown starts to surround him. As he thinks of breaking his pattern of immediately starting a new relationship when one ends to avoid being alone with all his uncomfortable feelings, he picks up the plaster applier with a trembling hand. Alone is Sam's unknown and he fears the pain he associates with it.

Sam has used other keys to get him to the point of peering through the crack in his egg, but how does he actually walk through? He doesn't...he leaps! It is like the Nike slogan. Just do it! He has already observed his pattern of rushing into a new relationship to avoid the pain of aloneness. He observed this without judgment (*NJSO Key*). He has already asked himself the question, "Could I do this, be alone?" (*Self-Questioning Key*). He knows it would take courage (*Courage Key*), and risk, (*Healthy-Risk Key*). Maybe before he leaps, he still needs more Keys on his chain. The *Change-of-Perspective Key*, when on his chain, can open up the way for him to see being alone differently, to see all the gifts time by himself and for himself might bring.

Sam walked through that crack. He waited eight months, a long time for Sam, before he started dating. He took a leap. Maybe he had yet another Key on his chain, one that enabled him to put the *Embrace-the-Unknown Key* into action. He used our next key, the *Self-Trust Key*.

SELF-TRUST KEY

This next Key, **Self-Trust**, like the ones that will follow, are keys needed to open some antique prisons. The prison of Lack of Self-Trust is a heavily reinforced prison. Many hands forged the bars and the lock is rusty. The good news is that, coupled with other Keys you already have on your keychain, the *Self-Trust Key* has enough teeth to finesse the most determined lock.

What is self-trust? It is a healthy self-connection, an honest knowing of who you are and who you are not. It is a belief in oneself, a self-validation. It is the belief that you can count on yourself. Trust is needed to have a healthy relationship with anyone. Self-trust is needed to have a healthy relationship with yourself.

How do you develop this necessary building block to a healthy self if the early foundation of your life taught you not to trust yourself, and continues to reinforce that teaching? What or who caused you to mistrust yourself in the first place? How can you revisit the circumstances that led to your self-distrust, in order to see things differently? How can you revise your old story and be able to use the *Self-Trust Key* to open your prison doors? The *Self-Questioning Key* will lead to answers.

As a Baby, toddler, and child you are dependent upon adults for your survival. This primal survival encompasses physical, emotional, and spiritual dependence. The opinions of these critical adults in your early life are taken as facts. If, at three-years-old, you are told you are a terrible person, stupid, or a burden, you don't take a breath and say, "Excuse me, but I think that is an incorrect assessment of who I am." If only!

A child repeatedly spoken to negatively now embodies these painful judgments, even if a knowing inner voice disagrees. This early, implicit dissidence is the cause of early self-distrust. The ability to form self-trust has been wounded; how often and how deeply will affect the length of the injury to self-trust.

As a child, you couldn't possibly know, with certainty, who you are and who you are not. You're developing and changing minute by minute. Your brain has to be at a certain stage of development to take in abstract concepts and to process information on a certain level. Knowing yourself takes a lifetime. As a child, you need to believe that your parents, or the significant adults in your life, are right and therefore can keep you safe and protect you. If it is an early choice in either believing yourself or believing the adult you count on for survival, it is imperative that you believe the adult. You cannot afford to trust yourself.

As you get older, other challenges to your self-trust arise. You were born into a family culture, with its set of rules, values, and rhythms. Your innate temperament and developing personality may, at times, be at odds with that culture. When you don't have the pre-ferred look, the shared interests, or the rhythm of the culture, you ask yourself, "What's wrong with me? Why don't I fit in? How can I trust the way I am when it's so different from my family?" At this stage of your life experience and development, these valuable ques-tions usually lead to only one answer: "Something is wrong with me. I can't trust my style, my likes and wants, my own rhythm." All this self-blame adds other wounds to your self-trust.

The battle for individuation, first ignited around the age of two, comes into full bloom in the teenage years. As a teenager, identifica-tion with your peers has a strong magnetic pull, but at the same time there is a voice inside you trying to be heard, that says, "I am me. I do know who I am, and maybe it's not who others say I should be." This voice knows who you are, but the voice is so weak. How do you strengthen that voice and quiet the voices of others so you can get connected to yourself, so you can learn and feel what's true for you? How can you trust that fragile voice and make your life decisions from its truth? For this all-important **Self-Trust Key** to be firmly in your hand and then be put to use, it needs the assistance of the other keys on your keychain. The *NJSO Key*, the *Self-Questioning Key*, the *Courage Key*, the *Healthy-Risk Key*, the *Patience Key*, and the *Change-of-Perspective Key* are your allies in taking the leap that will be required of you, to enable you to turn the *Self-Trust Key*.

Let's observe Carmen as she learns to trust herself and use the **Self-Trust Key** to unlock the door to her lifelong imprisonment in the Prison of Lack of Self-Trust.

Story

Carmen grew up in a family culture that was very protective of girls and demanded that Carmen conform to its idea of a safely structured life. Her family also adhered to the belief that children, from the age of zero to twenty-one, should be seen and rarely heard. And remember, parents are right, because they can't be wrong. This was her family credo.

This environment wasn't conducive to Carmen speaking her truth or having an opportunity to get to know her truth. Carmen had to trust others outside of herself when it came to making decisions. She didn't develop a relationship with herself, and she forgot to go inside to hear that knowing voice.

Carmen is in her junior year of high school. She wants to go to college. She's interested in speech therapy, because she greatly admires the therapist who helped her correct an embarrassing lisp. Carmen wants to help others overcome their speech impediments.

166

Her parents want her to go to a school close to home so she can live at home until she eventually marries. They say, "That's what girls in our family do." The collage visits and application process are about to begin. Carmen's speech therapist went to an excellent school in Boston, well respected for its speech therapy program. She believes Carmen would be comfortable with the small classes and the school environment. Her parents say they will not allow her to apply to the Boston school. Carmen is used to doing what they want, and usually finds a way to be okay with their decisions for her. Most of the time she doesn't even know if she wants something different. Except this time.

The voice inside her is getting louder and it is causing Carmen a great deal of conflict. Her parents have always done what's best for her. They often tell her this. They say they know best. How can Carmen possibly be right? How can she apply to the school in Boston? How can she trust herself?

Carmen starts to question herself, not realizing she has embraced the **Self-Questioning Key**, a step toward freedom. She starts an internal dialogue, long overdue, out of the desperation of her conflict. The fact that Carmen is aware of an inner conflict shows she is entertaining the notion that she could be right about what she needs. She asks, "Why do I so strongly feel this school is right for me? How can I tell my parents so they might at least listen to me? Why don't they want me to go away, besides their belief that girls in our family do it this way?" Her next question is, "What will happen if I try to do something my parents are against?" This question is the last one asked when deciding if a risk is a healthy risk (*#5: Are you aware of a possible worst-case scenario outcome?*). Carmen is worried what the worst-case scenario would be if she trusts herself and speaks up to her parents. Is it worth the risk? Once she starts asking herself questions, a floodgate opens and there is a silent understanding that she has opinions, and some can probably be trusted. "Why do I want this so much? Do I really want this so much?" With each question, she learns more about herself and who she is. This budding self-knowing is the foundation for building self-trust.

The **Courage Key** is allowing her to question her parents' decision and to examine her own right to have a contrary opinion. The **Change-of-Perspective Key** allows Carmen to entertain the idea that a child, a seventeen-year-old, can be heard as well as seen, and can have a dream of her own. The **NJSO Key** lets her explore this new perspective without the Negative Self-Talk of, "I'm being disrespectful. I'm being willful. I'm such an ungrateful child." Despite all the Keys clutched in her hand, Carmen is battling herself, her ingrained teachings, and her parents' version of loyalty.

Carmen sends for the application to the Boston school, ready to discuss her action with her parents. One hand holds her jingling Keychain, while the other holds the telephone number of a waiting speech therapist.

SELF-ESTEEM KEY

The *Self-Esteem Key* weighs heavy on the Keychain. It is very old, composed of fortified steel, and has numerous teeth. This is a formidable Key and is intricately linked with our last Key, **Self-Trust**.

What is self-esteem? According to the *Random House Dictionary of the English Language*, it is "An objective respect for, or favorable impression of oneself."[18] The essence of self-esteem is respect for yourself, a pride in yourself, and a satisfaction, for the most part, with who you are. It is the feeling you are "enough."

The feeling that "I'm not good enough" is so pervasive that it is the material for a multitude of prisons. The Key that counters that painful and damaging belief, the **Self-Esteem Key**, will open numerous prison doors and allow you to breathe the life-affirming air of "I'm good enough."

You come to earth with self-esteem. Usually, around the age of two, your self-esteem, unless crushed before that young age, is asserted left and right. Throughout the years, through words, actions, experiences, or limited perspective on those experiences, you get the message, that you're "not good enough." Because of limited coping skills or the conflict between your uniqueness and a more homogeneous environment, you continue to get the message that you're "not good enough." Assaults to self-esteem start long before you've heard the word spoken or knew its meaning. Once your "original esteem" is fractured, it takes the acquisition of several Keys for a process of rebuilding. In this process you can develop respect for yourself, and a healthy self-love.

How? In the following illustrative vignette, you'll see how the energy, when using multiple Keys, allows this old, steel, multi-toothed Key to be turned. What might have been a life sentence is now reprieved by the *Self-Esteem Key.*

Story

In our vignette, Jess has a very precocious sibling, Victor, who is two years his senior. His family expected Jess to be as quick to learn, as smart, and as curious as Victor. This comparison "set-up," started in Jess's home, and was carried into his school life. His teachers, who'd had precocious Victor two years earlier, expected another Victor. In never measuring up, Jess got the message that he definitely wasn't enough. Jess's own abilities were not recognized, and his uniqueness not seen or valued. It was hard for Jess to develop self-esteem without having a self. Jess was only seen in comparison to his brother Victor. His individuality was not recognized or validated.

When it was time to apply to colleges, Jess didn't apply to the schools he wanted to go to because he felt he wouldn't be accepted. He wasn't pushed to try. By this time in his life, Jess saw himself through a filter of "not enough" and it affected all his decisions. To escape the pain of comparison, Jess would go to the movies and to Broadway plays with his best friend Molly. Molly's father worked on Broadway and was able to get them tickets. Jess and Molly would write their own two-character, one-act plays and would have fun pretending to be their created characters when they had free time together.

Jess and Molly saw an ad for auditions that were being held by a respected local theater company. There was a part Molly thought would be perfect for Jess. Jess's first reaction, "I can't, I'm not good enough," didn't completely silence the voice inside that said, "I want this part; maybe I can." Here, his best friend Molly served as the **NJSO Key** to start Jess on his journey toward the **Self-Esteem Key**.

Molly pointed out to Jess how many roles they had seen played on both screen and stage, and how many Jess had created and played himself. She helped Jess remember how easily he got into a role, memorized lines, and enjoyed acting. She said Jess was talented and she thought he could, at the very least, try out for the part.

That night Jess used the *Self-Questioning Key* to see what the risk was if he tried out for the play and what he needed to do to take the risk. Jess was still too afraid because the risk of failure seemed too big. He was afraid to fail when his brother Victor was still succeeding at all he tried.

To continue to encourage Jess to overcome his fear, Molly shared her *Think-Out-of-the Box Key* with Jess. She suggested they rent the movie version of the play so Jess could get more comfortable with the part. Jess immediately biked to Barnes & Noble to get the DVD. Stimulated by the brain-storming of out-of-the-box thinking, Jess asked Molly if her father thought they could get a script of the play. Jess knew it was unlikely, but was now open to possibilities. He felt less afraid and was actively looking for ways to practice before the audition.

The two Keys that helped Jess take a leap toward building self-esteem were the *Change-of- Perspective Key,* and the *Self-Trust Key*. Because his best friend Molly had known him all of his life and knew his family dynamic, he was willing to listen to her point of view about him in relation to his brother Victor. The way she saw it was that Jess was not less than Victor, but rather he was different from him. Jess had never looked at it that way before, and that way of seeing himself in relation to his brother Victor was freeing. All day long he keeps telling himself, "I'm not less than Victor, I'm just different from Victor." Each time he said this it calmed and excited him at the same time. He decided he would say this to himself every morning when he got up and every night when he went to bed. After a few months, Jess began to feel, not just say, the words

Jess had his own interests, but never shared them with his family for fear they wouldn't be valued. With the help of some Keys and a compassionate friend, self-esteem was sprouting. Jess was beginning to consider auditioning for the part of Felix in the play *The Odd Couple*. Jess started to hear that inner voice, the one that really knew he could do this part: "This is about who you are, what you like, what you are good at; it has nothing to do with Victor." He noticed that his esteem was strengthened each time he gave credence to this inner voice.

Jess began to trust this new awareness, and with Molly's reinforcement, Jess was able to tentatively approach the **Self-Esteem Key**. This is a Key Jess holds strongly in his hand as he reads the glowing reviews, "Jess Pratt, a Feisty, Finicky Felix. We applaud his talent."

* * *

Take your time and take in the information given in this chapter. Decide if it applies to you and then put it into action.

Potential-Expansion Keys

Put a check(s) next to the Keys you feel you need:

- **The Optimize-Options Key** ____
- **The Embrace-the-Unknown Key** ____
- **The Self-Trust Key** ____
- **The Self-Esteem Key** ____

CHAPTER ELEVEN

Spirit Keys

- **The Self-Acceptance Key**
- **The Self-Forgiveness Key**
- **The Gratefulness Key**
- **The Presence Key**

These last four Keys are very heavy Keys, yet when you finally hold them in your hand you will feel lighter and freer than you have ever felt before. They are the Spirit Keys. The first two, the *Self-Acceptance Key* and the *Self-Forgiveness Key*, are so intertwined that they need to be discussed by flowing back and forth between them. Can you accept yourself without forgiving yourself? Can you forgive yourself without accepting yourself? The answer is yes...but

I think one without the other would lead to a very tenuous prison break with a good chance of recidivism. The *Gratefulness Key* opens you to an awareness of what is positive in your life. It frees you from the filter of negativity. This Key takes you beyond seeing the glass as half full or half empty. It frees you to see, even if the glass can only be viewed as half empty, that there is room for gratefulness. The *Presence Key* gives you the gift of conscious awareness. With it on your keychain you can experience the moment you are in and take an action based upon your present reality.

Each of these four Keys takes conscious work to acquire. Each can take a lifetime until you can use it with ease. It is worth it.

Once you have done the work and hold these Keys in your hand, your prison-building days are, for the most part, over. Your unconscious jailer immediately has to head for the unemployment line. Your prison breaks are 99.5% guaranteed to be successful.

If these four Keys are so powerful and effective, why bother with the other Keys? Because it is the work you've done to obtain the twelve other Keys that makes it possible for you to add these last four Keys to your chain. In this chapter, I am offering the Spirit Keys. These are the Keys of **Self-Acceptance**, **Self-Forgiveness**, **Gratefulness**, and **Presence**. It is now time to try them in the locks of your prisons.

SELF-ACCEPTANCE KEY

This is a golden Key. It's a Key that unlocks most prison doors. It's a Key that will enable you to use the other Keys in this chapter. That's the good news!

The less exhilarating news is that it takes a lot of conscious work on your part to develop the self-love, honesty, patience, and compassion needed to have a secure grip on this key. It is work that you will continue to do over your lifetime, with normal lapses into non-acceptance along the way.

The support of all the other Keys is necessary because this golden Key is the culmination of all the conscious work you did to acquire those twelve Keys. Once you have put the **Self-Esteem Key** on your keychain you are then able to make room for the *Self-Acceptance Key*. This Key, standing on the shoulders of all the Keys that have come before, is truly birthed from their synergy.

The great news is … you can do it!

The term self-acceptance is difficult to define because of the vastness of the word "self." In the Random House Dictionary of the English Language, words that define "self" are "complete individuality; a person's nature; the ego; the unity principle, as a soul."[20] What is meant by the word "self," in the **Self-Acceptance Key** is simply who you are and who you are not. What's not so simple is *acceptance.* Even after you discover who your self is, you still need to embrace the self-love, honesty, patience and compassion to accept that discovered self.

Similar conditions to those that contributed to your lack of self-trust and your lack of self-esteem contributed to your lack of self-acceptance. It is all part of an intricately woven tapestry. Going back to your early family life, many people let you know, verbally or through their actions, who they thought you were and who they thought you should be. You were introduced to their values, their beliefs, and their interests. You became aware of their subtle, or not-so-subtle, signals. From these signals you learned what 'about you' was unacceptable. This could have included your appearance, behavior, interests, needs, thoughts, or feelings. Needing your family for your survival, for your nurturance and approval, you adapted yourself to fit their views of what was all right for you to be. You became the "self" they accepted.

If this was not who you were, your attempts at trying to be that self could have led to confusion, failure, or anxiety. It could even have led to an unconscious disconnect from your "silenced" true self. On an unconscious level, the dissonance between who they wanted you to be and who you really were created a feeling of not-okayness. These were the beginnings of non-self -acceptance.

In the world of school, you met more people and had more experiences. You were no longer only influenced by family, you now had other role models to learn from. You started to gravitate towards your own interests, thoughts, feelings, and friends.

You might have started to tentatively question your family's evaluation of who they thought you were or should be. You were using the *Self-Questioning Key*, and the *Healthy-Risk Key* on this journey of self-discovery. While on this journey, you were bound to mess up occasionally. Whether the adopted version of yourself messed up, or your uncovered true self messed up, it could have been hard to accept these life mistakes. The bigger the mistake, the harder it was to accept it and to accept the self who did it. The more others were intolerant and judged you for making a mistake, the harder it was to accept yourself.

When you unconsciously move from guilt because you made a mistake, to shame because you think you *are* a mistake, it becomes nearly impossible to have self-acceptance. This is where we flow to the ***Self-Forgiveness Key***. This key can make acceptance of a mistake possible. Actually, it is needed for a more complete self-acceptance, and we will soon explore how it can be acquired.

How do you start on this long path to self-acceptance? This is a *key* question… and the answer is Keys! The following story of Tyler's path to self-acceptance will give life and breath to the journey for this golden Key.

Story

Tyler was a premature baby. He came into earth weighing only four-and-a-half pounds and had a small hole in his little heart. Tyler was the first successful birth after his mother and father's experience of two miscarriages. He was also the first grandson in the family.

Tyler was very protected by his parents. His safety was uppermost in their minds, and in their choices for Tyler. His grandparents treated him like a King—carrier of their family name, heir to the throne. The stage was set for an overprotected and revered child, who learned at an early age that the way to take care of his family was to take care of himself.

Although Tyler grew up safe and very loved by his family, he also grew up lonely. He had the distinct feeling that he didn't fit in, that he was different from other kids his age. The difference made him somehow less-than. His parents told him that he couldn't play sports because he had been born with a hole in his heart. What they failed to tell him was that the hole had been fixed before he even left the hospital, and that the doctors said he was therefore as healthy as anyone. Tyler was actually able to play the sports he longed to play. Tyler's parents loved him very much and were petrified they could lose him. They didn't believe what the doctors had said and still believed that the hole in his heart, though fixed, was a danger to Tyler's health. Tyler started to see himself as fragile and unhealthy, and his esteem was not buoyed by his family's love.

When Tyler was twelve, his grandfather started to groom him to one day take over his successful furniture business. Since Tyler wasn't on any sports team, every Saturday he and his grandfather traveled by train to the furniture store. After six years of Saturdays, Tyler knew the business and knew he wasn't interested in running it. Tyler felt this news would devastate his grandfather. He felt guilty for being so ungrateful. Tyler clearly knew what he didn't want to do, but he still didn't know what he did want to do. He had never made his own choices, and he had never let himself wonder what he liked or wanted. He lived in a locked box of safety and he had no idea who he was.

Tyler felt desperate because he knew that soon his grandfather would officially ask him to start working at the store so he could learn all aspects of the business. Tyler, now eighteen, had not been directed towards college and he had little to fall back upon. In desperation, he started to ask himself some questions. He picked up the **Self-Questioning Key** to clear some of the chaos in his mind.

"What do I like? I must like something. What am I good at? I must be good at something." Tyler found a quiet space outside of his home to think. The **Courage Key** and the **Patience Key** then allowed Tyler to sit through his agitation while exploring this unfamiliar territory of self-awareness.

"I like trains," was the answer that bubbled up. "What kid doesn't? But I think I like them more." Tyler answered his own questions.

Every Saturday, Tyler and his grandfather rode to the store in an empty train. This gave Tyler an opportunity to get to know the conductor and to ride next to the locomotive engineer on many of his trips. This was his favorite part of the six years of Saturdays. During those six years he had used the Internet to learn about trains and the jobs of conductor and locomotive engineers. He learned about the training, the experience and the other qualifications for each job.

He started to go to all the train shows and he had every Lionel train made. His parents encouraged his hobby because it was safe and it distracted Tyler from his upset over not playing team sports, or going to sleepovers, or taking part in activities his parents considered unsafe.

Tyler tried to play down his passion because it only made him feel more different. He couldn't accept this self, a self that had this interest, and a self that didn't want what his parents and grandparents wanted for him. A self that was afraid to trust himself.

One Friday night his grandfather told Tyler he'd like to go for breakfast the next morning before they took the train to the store. Tyler knew his grandfather would ask the dreaded question.

That night, as he lay awake in his bed, he was able to stay quiet enough to step back and observe himself. In a moment of non-judgment (*NJSO Key*) he saw the truth of his desire to be a locomotive engineer and the truth of his dislike of the furniture business.

He clutched the *Courage Key* and *Healthy-Risk Key* in his sweaty hand as he rehearsed what he would say to his grandfather.

To decide if speaking to his grandfather was a healthy risk to take, he asked himself the questions that would help him make that decision. He was filled with anxiety when he asked, "What is the worst that can happen if I tell my grandfather I don't want to run his business? He might not like me. He might be so upset that he gets sick. He might not talk to me." Tyler realized that even if these things happened, he could not sit in the furniture store and keep the books and sell things he didn't care about. He took a deep breath and put the **Embrace-the-Unknown Key** under his pillow. As he was falling asleep he had a thought he hadn't allowed himself before, "Maybe it's *okay* to want this. Maybe it's an *okay* job." The **Change-of-Perspective Key** was available to his unconscious as he drifted off to sleep. Waking up in the middle of the night, he used the **Patience Key** to stop himself from calling his grandfather and to wait until morning for the right time to speak his truth.

In the morning, still clutching the **Courage Key**, he felt afraid but at the same time he felt afraid, he felt a glimmer of pride that he was finally going to speak up. He knew, in his gut, that his grandfather was going to ask him to run the business. That's what this morning's breakfast was all about. He was going to tell his grandfather the truth even though he didn't know how his grandfather would react. In the midst of his fear, Tyler had moments of calmness. After courageously asking himself some hard questions and answering them truthfully, he was beginning to trust himself. Tyler's keychain was getting heavier. He was holding the **NJSO Key**, the **Self-Questioning Key**, the **Courage Key**, the **Embrace-the-Unknown Key**, the **Healthy-Risk Key**, *the* **Change-of-Perspective Key**, and the **Success- in-Trying Key**.

Tyler's grandfather was silent for what seemed like eons after Tyler told him about his dreams, and all the information he had gathered from the Internet and from Walt, their locomotive engineer. Finally, his grandfather spoke. He said he had been planning to ask Tyler to run the business. He said how disappointed he was, but he'd had a feeling Tyler wasn't interested in running the store. He told Tyler that he wanted him to be as happy in what he did for a living as he himself was in his business. They talked about Tyler's information on the education, training, and experience needed to become a locomotive engineer. He suggested they go to Walt's station and talk to him about the realities of the job, not Tyler's dream of the job.

Tyler couldn't believe how well his grandfather handled the news. He couldn't believe his grandfather supported his dreams. This support was the piece Tyler needed to strengthen his newly forming self-trust, and his budding self-esteem.

The leap, while holding all these Keys in his hand to self-acceptance, was freeing. Tyler was filled, with a deep okayness for the first time in his life, in every cell and pore of his body. He was able to breathe in who he was and breathe out who he wasn't.

Tyler was now genuinely safe. Not because of the external protection of his parents, but because the internal protection of his new self-acceptance freed him to live a genuine life.

SELF-FORGIVENESS KEY

The last Key you tried, the **Self-Acceptance Key**, is a necessary partner if you are to own the **Self-Forgiveness Key**. Even if you have a reasonable level of self-acceptance, this can be a difficult Key to keep a firm grasp on. In a world that has the technology, the intelligence, and the drive to put men on the moon, why are so many people still imprisoned by their inability to forgive themselves?

What makes this Key so difficult to possess? Because you are often unaware that there is something you don't forgive yourself for. This unawareness makes it impossible to take action. You can't put effort into finding a Key to a prison you don't know you're in.

Once you realize the need to forgive yourself, you realize it is one of the hardest things that you will ever have to do. A clue to the evolvement of those who were able to use the **Self-Forgiveness Key** is found in the well-known phrase, "To err is human; to forgive, divine."[21] This is a daunting statement. With the **Change-of-Perspective Key** and The **Think-Out-of-the-Box Key** in my hand, I'll invoke poetic license and revise the phrase. "To err is humane; to forgive is *really, really hard work.*"

How does non-self-forgiveness imprison you? When you don't forgive yourself, you are living with the pain of self-judgment. You have decided that what you said, or did, or didn't do, was so bad that it is impossible to forgive yourself. When you generalize this non-forgiveness, and your Negative Self-Talk reinforces this generalized "badness," your life and your life choices become filtered through that perception. If you believe that you are in some way bad, and therefore undeserving, your unhealthy relationship choices and your ineffective goal-setting methods are a reflection of this harmful belief.

As redundant as it may sound, the *NJSO Key*, and *Self-Questioning Key* will set you free! It can be difficult to step back with a healthy detachment and ask, "Did I say that/ do that/ not do that because I'm mean, because I'm conniving, or because I'm lazy? Could there be other reasons for what I said/ did/ didn't do that are less heinous? Would I condemn someone else for this same crime without seeing the bigger picture in which the unforgivable occurred? Could I have done it differently?"

Stepping back and self-questioning to broaden your scope of observation is a way to show compassion for yourself. It's not always easy to do, but it's worth it! Through questioning, you are using the *Change-of-Perspective Key* to open up the possibility of seeing things differently.

If you are willing to walk down the path of self-forgiveness, the *Think-Out-of-the-Box Key* and the *Optimize-Your-Options Key* could move you many paces ahead.

Instead of using only self-talk to convince yourself that you deserve self-forgiveness (although self-talk is a very powerful tool), you could also read books on the subject, listen to tapes, pray, and hand it over to something greater than yourself. You could ask the people that were able to accomplish this daunting task of self-forgiveness about the methods that they used. You can start the process by forgiving yourself for a very small transgression. The ability to do this on a small scale will strengthen your self-esteem, your self-trust, and your self-acceptance. It will pave the way for you to forgive yourself on a larger scale.

In my personal quest for self-forgiveness, I was forced to think out of the box and came upon a discussion on a tape that opened me up to self-forgiveness. I listened to this tape over twenty years ago, I don't remember the name of the tape, or even the main subject matter. I remember the essence of what was said, and it had a profound effect on my journey towards self-forgiveness.

"You can forgive yourself because the person you were, at the time of your unforgivable action or inaction, was a person incapable of making a different choice." That "you" was made up of all that came before your "moment of terrible choice": your innate personality, your family life (nature and nurture), and the sum total of all your experiences. So at that moment, the person formed by all those components couldn't have done it differently.

Use the **Patience Key** on your chain and reread this several times. Use the **Change-of-Perspective Key**. Is it possible for you to see it this way?

So I realized, that even though the person I am today wouldn't have make the same choice, I did do things in the past that I wasn't proud of. After acknowledging this, and after feeling all my sadness around it, I did forgive myself, and freed myself from a long-term, self-imposed imprisonment. I honestly believe that the person I was then couldn't have made another choice. It's not an excuse; it's a sad and painful fact.

Those few lines on a tape that I happened to listen to, perhaps for a different purpose, has brought me peace. It enabled me to forgive myself and at the same time accept myself with all my many imperfections.

If you are willing to start on the road to self-forgiveness, hold your full keychain in your hand and ask yourself the following questions. You are worth the effort and courage it takes to ask important questions that can lead you to a truth that is freeing:

1) Could there be something I need to forgive myself for?

2) Am I able to see what I said/ what I did/ what I didn't do that I identify as unforgivable in another way?

3) Was I capable, being who I was at the time, of doing it differently?

4) If the answer to No. 3 is "Yes," then ask, "If I could have, why didn't I?"

5) Would I forgive someone else who said/ did/ didn't do this?

6) Would I do this today?

7) If I still can't forgive myself, can I ask myself these questions again in three months? (Use The *Patience Key*, *Success-in-Trying Key*, *Healthy-Risk Key*).

The state of grace produced when you've found the *Self-Forgiveness Key* is a state of mind that guides you to our next Key, the *Gratefulness Key*.

GRATEFULNESS KEY

This Key has many qualities. It is first and foremost a memory stimulator. It is a balancer. It is a powerful energy that can lift mild depression, calm anxiety, and bring a quiet smile to smileless lips.

Each Key is unique, and each has elements in common with all the other Keys. As is true for all the other Keys, to make this very precious *Gratefulness Key* available to you, you need to develop the ability to be in a state of awareness. It's easier said than done, because of the strong pull to unawareness.

Why would you want to stay unaware? Let me count the reasons. Unawareness is the avoidance technique of choice for many people. It is used as a means of avoiding that which you cannot bear to see. It helps you avoid the pain of knowing. The irony is that the pain eventually caused by your continued unawareness is, in the long run, far greater than the pain you were initially avoiding.

Who would want to see your child changing before your eyes? "He seems to have switched friends," you think to yourself. "He has fits of rage, my gentle Mikey, and things seem to be missing around the house." Who would want to see your parent seeming to forget her appointments, leaving the oven on, looking unkempt? "Mom has always been so meticulous." The most frightening change is that she's forgetting your name. Who would want to see your partner's loss of appetite, tiredness, and fearful eyes?

The answer to all three questions is: no one. But, if you don't see the truth of these three examples, the situation will only worsen. Having the *Courage Key*, enabling you to see the truth, gives you the opportunity to take action, to ameliorate the circumstances, or to even reverse them. Yes, there is much pain in the awareness that your child has a serious drug problem, that your parent has dementia, or

186

Alzheimer's disease, or that your partner is very ill. On one level, the avoidance of awareness makes perfect sense; it is protective. And if your awareness is challenged before you are ready or able to see, denial comes to your rescue. Denial was one of those "forts" of childhood, a protector and coping mechanism used when you had few others. When you were a child, denial was your friend. It worked by keeping you from seeing what was intolerable and what you couldn't change. But if you, as an adult keep the fort as your only coping mechanism, at some point, you become imprisoned. A prison, while it keeps painful feelings at bay, also keeps awareness of reality at bay. The ability to make decisions based upon the reality is therefore impossible. The pain of seeing can be considered the "negative side" of awareness.

On the positive side, awareness is a powerful change agent. There can be no change without awareness. It is the quintessential first step! Like your first step when you were a baby, it can be a long time in coming, but once taken, many steps follow. Each small step takes you where you want to go. While clutching your **Courage Key** you can begin to embrace the awareness needed before you can experience true gratefulness.

To be grateful is to appreciate. Simple? It can be. First you need the awareness, then some Keys to unlock the gifts that awareness holds. A flashlight, or other light source can help to shine light during dark times while looking for gratefulness. It is important to say that gratefulness is not just another method of denial. You see and say to yourself that something is truly bad, sad, painful, and unfair, and even though this is so, there can still be some awareness of other reasons for gratefulness. Your feelings are valid. Deep feelings you have as a result of certain painful experiences can't be rushed along. They demand time.

The *Gratefulness Key* adds *to* the "divine tingle" of the chain. Many other Keys have led the way to finding this Spirit Key: The *Patience Key*, the *Self-Questioning Key*, the *Change-of-Perspective Key*, the ubiquitous *Courage Key*, and the *Self-Acceptance Key* have forged the way.

With awareness you can ask yourself, "What am I grateful for? If the circumstances of my present life are nothing I feel grateful about, can I remember a time when there was reason to feel grateful? In some bad situations (*Change-of-Perspective Key*) was there still reason for gratefulness, now that I have the 20/20 vision of hindsight?" (*Self-Questioning Key*). "What would I put on a list, or just say to myself in the morning to help me balance the negative things happening in my life, to help me with the depression I feel every morning, to help me remember there really are some things I can still feel grateful about? Can I create my own gratefulness affirmation to set a positive tone to my day?"

When trying to find reasons to be grateful, use your memories of the past as well as your awareness of the present. You might only be able to approach the past being grateful for what didn't happen. There may be a few things to be grateful for: "I am grateful for my aunt, grandma, cousin, Darrell, Sima, and Mrs. Novak. I'm grateful I was a fast runner, good speller, not noticed." The search for gratefulness can be facilitated if you first make a list of all the things you realize you take for granted and move them over to your gratefulness list. "I am grateful I can breathe with ease, I am grateful I can hear, see, smell, taste, and touch. I am grateful I can walk, speak, swallow, go to the bathroom, and that I'm not in continuous physical, mental, emotional and spiritual pain."

In the morning, if you think about who you will interact with during the day, are you grateful for any of those people? Are you grateful that you have, if you do, a job? Money for food? Clothing and shelter? The ability to pay your bills?

Are you grateful for your ability to appreciate the beauty of a flower, the graceful swoop of a bird, the warmth of the sun, and the flitting of a butterfly's wing? Can you, with the *NJSO Key* close by, become aware of who you are and who you aren't (*Self-Acceptance Key*)? Be grateful that you have a sense of humor/ that you can finish what you start/ that you can meet commitments you make/ that you make a mean lasagna/ that you can apologize when you're wrong? Can you be grateful that you are a person who cares about people, or animals, or a cause, or your appearance, or your religious beliefs? Are you grateful that you are grateful?

Why is gratefulness worth developing? Because when you experience gratefulness there is a peace available to you, a freedom never before yours.

In order to get to the *Gratefulness Key*, you need to use other Keys first. The *Self-Questioning Key* helps to jog your memory to remember what has been good in your life. The *Change-of-Perspective Key* affords you the distance and perspective to see situations and people in a different way, one that shows why you can be grateful for these situations and these people. The same Key creates space for a mind shift, from what you took for granted to what is a reason for gratefulness. With the *NJSO Key* on your keychain you can take a non-judgmental inventory of yourself, finding some five things about yourself to be grateful for.

The *Gratefulness Key* gives you a chance to take a breath and to quiet yourself. It allows you to put life in perspective; it balances the good and the bad. The *Gratefulness Key* is a reminder to look around you and to look inside yourself with an unwavering aware-ness, and to see all of the gifts, both large and small, that are reasons to be grateful. It is a gentle Key with the strength to open many prison doors.

PRESENCE KEY

The *Presence Key* unlocks within you a deep sense of inner freedom. The *Presence Key* lets you access a level of alertness that makes all things possible. When you hold the *Presence Key*, all other Keys can be used to their fullest potential. It is a Key you want on your keychain.

What is presence? It is being in the moment; total consciousness in the moment. What's so hard about that? What could possibly keep you from being in the present moment? (Are you smiling as you read this?)

Is there danger in being present? Once again, you need to look back at your life to see yourself as a child, devoid of a multitude of coping skills. You needed the fort of "I shall not see," or "I shall not be" for important self-protection. Did the coping skills of not being aware and not being present keep you safe and alive as a child? If so, as an adult, you would believe that denial and unawareness are needed in times of unbearable pain.

Denial, selective unawareness, and non-presence are welcome friends, to a point. Past this point, these friends turn into prisons and greatly limit your ability to receive the important gifts that only presence can offer. Some of these gifts are: the gift of conscious choice; the gift of knowing you can handle pain; the gift of knowing that you can take life-affirming actions for yourself; and the gift of knowing you are able to do what you need to do.

In the classrooms where I went to elementary school, every morning was a routine. I now see this as brilliant. During that routine of taking of *attendance*: Johnny...present; Gilda...present; Oscar... present," we were subtly called to awareness. We were each brought back from wherever our minds had roamed. We then, at least, had the presence of mind needed to be able to learn.

At the beginning of workshops that I facilitate, I always tell the group, "Raise your hand if you're here." At first everybody looks confused. Then someone laughs, and someone else smiles, and one by one they start to raise their hands. They need to be present to get the information they came to get. Some are still thinking about what happened before they arrived—a conversation, a situation, or what will happen later—the dinner they'll eat or who they'll be meeting at three o'clock.

How does the **Presence Key** set you free? How do you get hold of this key that offers inner peace? No one is free who is locked into the past or locked into the future. The past and the future keep you from being fully alive, because life is only happening in the present moment. Change can only happen in the present.

The only way you can impact the past is in the present. In the present moment, you can consciously decide to change your attitude toward what happened in the past. But you need the presence of mind to realize that a change of attitude is needed. This change of attitude will benefit your health and well-being by freeing you from the prison of the past. This frees you to see the reality in front of you. You need to see reality in order to make healthy life choices.

The only way you can impact the future is by making conscious choices, in the present moment, about what you would like to have happen. Once you have a good enough idea of what you'd like to occur in the future, you can make plans and set goals for that future. The future will get here even if you make no plans. If, in the present, you make a conscious plan based on the reality you can now see, you increase affecting your desired outcome. As Jack Nicholson's character said in *One Flew Over the Cuckoo's Nest*, you can say "At least I tried."

Being present in the moment frees you to participate in healthy communication with the people in your life. So many couples I have seen through the years list poor communication as a big source of their problems. Many people desire to be understood. People would love to be agreed with, but if not, at least understood. The statements, "He doesn't listen to me," and the statement "I didn't say that. How'd she get that from what I said?" reflect these misunderstandings.

You can't listen to someone if you're not in the present moment when they're talking to you. Maybe you don't want to hear what they're saying, or how they're saying it, or that it has been said a thousand times before. Not being present is a defense.

If, on the other hand you want the relationship to get better, if you want to honor the other person by truly listening, presence is the Key. You need to be present for a continued dialogue, based upon what the other person is saying happened. The **Presence Key** frees you from unnecessary misunderstandings and from hurting someone you care about when your non-presence is experienced as indifference.

Presence can be calming. It can reduce the stress of anxiety over thoughts of the past, or fears of the unknown future. It can allow you to take in the sights and smells and sounds of your surroundings, and to experience the joy and the beauty and the companionship around you. You can breathe in the energy of a fully alive moment.

The **Presence Key** is available to you every moment you consciously choose to embrace it, to hold it in your hand. The **Self-Questioning** Key is a dominant Key in active pursuit of presence.

Remembering to ask, "Am I here?" is a simple, yet powerful way to bring you back to the present moment where all opportunities await.

You can use the **Healthy-Risk Key** when deciding if staying present, in a particular situation, with a particular person, is worth the risk. The **Courage Key** assists you in being present in situations you have assessed are important and need your presence to be handled. Before having the **Presence Key**, you might have hidden from this situation by using your old friend, non-presence, as a protector.

The **Patience Key** joins the **Courage Key** in helping you accept failed attempts you make to stay present in a painful moment. The **Success-in-Trying Key** adds its support. While you learn to embrace the calming state of "presence," the **NJSO Key** remains firmly in your hand.

If you are willing to practice asking yourself, a few times a day, "Am I present?" and willing to bring yourself back to the present when you know you have drifted, you will start to experience the inner freedom this Key promises.

Take your time and digest the information given in this chapter. Decide how it applies to you and then to put it into action. You now have a full keychain. You have the Keys available to free you from your self-perpetuated prisons. Awareness is the first step to all change. The Keys are ready to open all the locks, but only you can turn the Keys.

In the next chapter we will follow the stories of five people, playing their unconscious roles of Prisoner, Prison Builder, Jailer, and finally conscious Key Holder. Each story culminates in a well-earned Prison Break.

Spirit Keys

Put a check(s) next to the Keys you feel you need:

- **The Self-Acceptance Key** _____
- **The Self-Forgiveness Key** _____
- **The Gratefulness Key** _____
- **The Presence Key** _____

Part V

Prison Breaks

CHAPTER TWELVE

Five Prison Break Stories

If not now, when? It is finally time for your Prison Break! You started your life as a builder of protective forts. At one point you became a Prisoner and then unconsciously morphed into a Prison Builder. Your continued unconsciousness made you the perfect candidate for your role as vigilant jailer. Perhaps in your moments of consciousness, you eyed the shining, tinkling Keys on that big keychain hanging from the Jailer's belt. Maybe you even plotted how to get one of those Keys and use it to unlock your cell door.

But the unknown of freedom was a frightening concept. Who would you be? What choices would you be faced with? Could you envision a self who's not ruled by what others want you to be? Could you imagine living a genuine life?

This section tells five Prison Break stories. You have already been introduced to the main character of each story in a previous vignette. In their expanded stories, I have repeated sections of text from their individual stories, which have been placed throughout the book. Repetition is an excellent method of teaching, because repetition reinforces what has been learned. The repetition is used to reinforce awareness of how each character became a Prisoner, what Prisons he or she built, who his or her vigilant Jailers were as well as what Keys each used for a Prison Break. The five main characters are at a point in their personal process of evolution at which they are ready to break free. Something deep inside them is screaming for the life of their very souls. The soul is that part of them that enters earth knowing who they are, accepting who they are, and loving who they are. It's now, or possibly never.

Let's look at each of their stories from the early Fort Builder, then Prisoner, Prison Builder, and unconscious Jailer roles, all the way to their well-earned victory as Key Holders. Their prison breaks were only possible by each using his or her unique combination of Keys.

Tessa, Mike, Hannah, Devon and Bess are giving you a gift. They are modeling how a Prison Break can succeed and how you can be Your Own Worst Enemy…No More! The Prison Break Model at the end of each story puts in outline form how each character became a Prisoner, what Prisons were built, what Jailers kept him or her imprisoned, and finally what combination of Keys each used for a life-affirming Prison Break. By answering the questions at the end of each chapter you have been creating your own Prison Break Model. Fill in the form at the end of the five Prison Break stories with all of your accumulated checks ☑.

Prison Break Story No. 1: Tessa Giovanni

Tessa is the subject of our first Prison Break story. You were briefly introduced to her in Chapter Two, on Unhealthy Relationship Choices. We will follow Tessa's unique path from early Fort Builder to Prison Builder, to Jailer and finally Key Holder, when she joyously unlocks her prison doors!

Tessa Marisa Giovanni had four siblings. When she was two years old, her mother was in the middle of a life-threatening sixth pregnancy. Her twelve-year-old sister, Anita, was given the role of Tessa's "mother" while her father, grandparents, and aunt handled the other children and household responsibilities.

Tessa was a normal two-year-old and her favorite and much repeated words were "No," and "Me do!" She was at the developmental stage of asserting her independence. To the Giovanni household, whose threshold of stress was at the max, Tessa's "No's" were intolerable. All little Tessa, the natural explorer, heard was, "Tessa, don't do that! Tessa, that's not how you do it!" No one had the time or patience to teach her how to do something or to encourage her two-year-old curiosity. She learned that everything she tried to do was wrong, and her unconscious mind began whispering, "You're not good enough, Tessa." So, at the ripe old age of five, she stopped trying.

Although her mother recovered, she lost the baby and spiraled into a deep depression that lasted three years. Tessa felt constantly rejected in each of her attempts to be close to her mother and to get the nurturing she craved. Now, her **Negative Self-Talk: I'm Not good Enough, I'll Never Be**, was happening on both a conscious and unconscious level. To her young mind, if her mother rejected her, she must not be enough. Tessa was still too young to verbalize her thoughts and feelings, and her family was still too caught up in crisis mode to notice Tessa's visible pain. By the time she was approaching six years old, she was convinced she was not good enough to be nurtured.

When Tessa was ten, her mother, who had been in better mental health over the last four years, went into another depression over the death of her mother. This new death triggered unresolved grief over her miscarriage of eight years ago. Again Tessa experienced painful rejection from her mother, who, over the last four years, had been able to give some nurturance to Tessa. At this time, Tessa still hadn't developed coping skills to help her survive the loss of maternal nurturance.

To survive the repeated loss of life-affirming nurturance, Tessa re-fortified her childhood forts. This re-fortification ingrained in her the unhealthy protective behaviors of self-judgment, and of being "too nice." They would soon become the materials of Tessa's same-named Prisons.

Tessa, as always, tried not to make waves. She tried hard to be "nice" to everybody. Because Tessa gave everybody just what they wanted, she got positive responses and she had glimpses of what being "good enough" could feel like. Unfortunately, the price was high. She had to continually bury the spirit of her feisty two-year-old self deep under her protective **Fort of Too Nice**.

The old painful criticisms that her family had inflicted on Tessa were now self-inflicted. Fifteen-year-old Tessa now told herself, "I can't do anything right." "My mother doesn't love me, she doesn't want me." Tessa became a master at self-judgment. This was much less painful than letting her family pass judgment. This second protective fort, by constant reinforcement, would soon develop into the **Prison of Self-Judgment**.

Tessa was smart. She did well in school but wouldn't try out for any sports teams, or school plays, or join any clubs. This pattern of not trying, of keeping her world small, was yet another prison she unconsciously built: the **Prison of Unhealthy-Patterns**.

Tessa was convinced she was "not good enough" and would fail at whatever she did. She saw herself as a flawed being and felt ashamed. Tessa also lived in one of the most painful Prisons, the **Prison of Shame**.

Her early protective forts had morphed into prisons by the time she was in High School. Tessa was unaware of the origins of why she felt as she did about herself and of why she kept her world so small. Her lack of consciousness made it impossible for her to question the truth of her adopted beliefs.

In her junior year of high school Tessa had an Italian teacher, Mrs. Ranice, who encouraged Tessa's natural ability with languages. She suggested Tessa take a second language the following year and apply to be an exchange student in Venice that coming summer. It was hard for Tessa to believe that someone thought she was good at something and for a breath-holding moment she had a flicker of self-esteem.

Tessa couldn't get up the courage to ask her family if she could apply to be an exchange student. The **Prison of Avoidance of Pain** was now being unconsciously added to young Tessa's Prison system. She told Mrs. Ranice that she couldn't go to Italy that summer but that she would think about taking a second language next year.

Tessa's guidance counselor helped her fill out applications for local colleges, and she was accepted to four out of six of them. It was hard for Tessa to acknowledge that she was good enough to be accepted to four colleges. Even with her family's rare praise, Tessa's unconscious Jailer took over to keep her imprisoned. Tessa could easily have been the author of four or five of the Jailer Resumes. The main trait of "Jailer-hood" is unconsciousness; so Tess would never realize that she could, in fact, be **Peter Fog,** whose resume states that he specializes in Negative Self-Talk and in keeping alive shame from the past. Tessa could also be resume writer **Maria Cant.** Maria is an astute reminder of what we can't do, and of the dangers of change. Tessa's pseudonym could even be **Kim Patterson**, the maker of historic patterns as a life model, or **Hugo First,** who is so nice and puts people in front of himself to the point of invisibility. Tessa's vigilant jailers softly speak to her whenever she allows herself to see and feel her value, and when her prison walls begin to crack. A crack in Tessa's Prison wall would immediately be fixed by **Jason Wall.** Jason is another Jailer whose resume suggests possible authorship by Tessa.

While in college, Tessa met Charlie. Not healthy herself at this point in her life, Tessa made an Unhealthy Relationship Choice. She chose someone who reinforces her own Negative Self-Talk. The three components of making yourself a prisoner are Negative Self-Talk, Unhealthy Relationship Choices, and Goal-Setting "setups." At twenty years of age, Tessa had two of the three. The third was not far behind.

Charlie, six years older than Tessa, initially made Tessa feel looked after, and finally nurtured. This was very important to Tessa and blinded her to an awareness that Charlie was, first, and foremost, a Reinforcer of her Negative Self-Talk, especially "I'm not good enough." At the beginning of their relationship, Charlie's suggestions seemed like constructive criticism. When he pointed out what she was doing wrong, he presented it as a friendly piece of advice from someone older and more experienced, who cared about her welfare.

When Charlie decided, after only six months into the relationship, that they should live together, Tessa, to please him, agreed. Tessa had set no goals for the relationship. Her lack of goal- setting made her easy prey to the **Goal-Setting Setup No. 2 : You Try to Meet a Goal Someone Else Set for You.** Soon after they moved in together, his advice became more forceful and he made it clear that Tessa had problems. Charlie said, in so many ways, that she wasn't enough: tall enough, slim enough, clever enough, attentive enough etc. He reinforced her ingrained belief that she wasn't good enough and he partnered with Tessa's unconscious jailers to keep her a prisoner. Charlie was a Reinforcer. Tessa had made **Unhealthy Relationship Choice No. 4.**

We have followed Tessa's journey so far from early Fort Builder, Prisoner, Prison Builder, and unconscious Jailer. In Tessa's fourth year of college, events occurred that forced her see herself as imprisoned. Those events put her on the path to finding her Prison Break keys.

A month before Tessa's college graduation, her father was killed in a tragic accident. It was a hit-and-run three blocks from their home. Just two weeks prior to this tragedy, Charlie sprang on Tessa that he wanted to move three thousand miles away from where they presently lived. He told Tessa he had been sending resumes and had an interview in two weeks. Charlie had never checked with Tessa. He told her she was bad when it came to making decisions, so he'd made the decision for them.

The third straw, the one that can tip life's balance and create "a dangerous opportunity," was the news that Tessa had been accepted into a four-year graduate program in Italy that combined a Masters and a Doctorate degree in languages. The chairman of her department had recommended Tessa for this golden opportunity. Tessa never thought that she had a chance of being accepted. She still thought that she wasn't good enough. She had put away any hope of being accepted so deeply that it was no longer available to her conscious mind.

Life's stage was now set for Tessa to recreate herself. Tessa had to allow to die the self that thought she wasn't good enough, that had for so long given away its personal power, and that had no voice.

Tessa couldn't sleep after Charlie's pronouncement. He kept insisting that she needed him and that she couldn't do life on her own. He told her daily that he had supported her while she went to school and now it was time for her to be supportive of him and do what he needed. Charlie was always kicking Tessa in her Achilles heel, which was her ingrained belief in her inadequacy. This old version of herself held fast, even with the great success of being accepted into this prestigious program.

Tessa was sleepless over Charlie's demands and the familiar pull she felt to please him (**Prison of Too Nice**). She was sleepless over the pull in opposite directions, toward the opportunity to study in Italy, to please her professors, and finally herself. The sleeplessness turned into a full-blown panic attack when her father was killed. Since Tessa was the only single sibling, all her brothers and sisters decided (they were not used to including Tessa in decision-making), that she should move back home for a while to help their fragile mother adjust to her loss. Tessa's mother had been prone to depression as a response to loss, so it seemed likely that she would be in need of help. This was a chance for Tessa to save her mother and in return receive the love she had craved her entire life. Her universe was cracking open and this time her unconscious Jailer (**Jason Wall**) might not have enough mortar for the repair.

Mrs. Ranice had stayed in touch with her gifted student. She called Tessa the moment she heard of her father's sudden and tragic death. Mrs. Ranice went to Tessa's apartment when she heard the panic in her voice, put her in the car and drove her back to her home for a cup of tea and the gift of a neutral and compassionate ear. It took the *Courage Key* for Tessa to risk telling Mrs. Racine the desperate need she had for her mother's love and for the love and support of Charlie. Because Mrs. Racine responded to her story without criticism or blame, Tessa was able, maybe for the first time in her life, to relax and drink in the comfort of being listened to without harsh judgment.

She expressed to Mrs. Racine that she didn't think she could make the decisions she was facing. She always tried to please everyone, but now she couldn't please her mother and siblings, Charlie, and her professors. All at once they wanted her to do conflicting things. She literally panicked, and as she continued to talk about this seemingly impossible conflict, her heart started to race, her hands shook and her legs felt weak. She panicked because it was impossible to make a decision that would please each of the people involved. The real battle, not yet realized by Tessa, was the battle her Prisons and Jailers were fighting to survive the threat from the first traces of consciousness emerging in Tessa, and the faint sound of jangling Keys.

As Mrs. Racine poured more tea, she asked Tessa two questions. Her questions startled Tessa. "What would please you, Tessa? What do *you* want?" Tessa couldn't answer the questions. She wasn't used to considering her own needs and wants. Mrs. Racine invited Tessa to stay in her guest room for a few days, away from the divergent needs of the people involved in each choice and from the high level of emotions that kept Tessa in panic mode.

Once in this quiet environment, Tessa tried to picture herself back in her parents' home, across the country with Charlie or in the university in Italy. It was alien for her to listen to her own thoughts, not overlaid with the wishes of others. It was difficult for Tessa to find her own voice and tune in to her own sensory signals. She had to struggle to keep the *NJSO Key* in hand while looking honestly at herself, her wants, and her needs. This was only the second time she had used **the *NJSO Key***. The first time was only for a moment in high school, when she took in Mrs. Racine's validation of her natural ability with languages.

On the fourth day at Mrs. Racine's home, Tessa noticed it was peaceful not to hear Charlie's voice telling her what she couldn't do. In the quiet and safety of Mrs. Racine's home, she was beginning to have the courage to see that their relationship was all about Charlie's needs. On day six at Mrs. Racine's, Tessa had a revelation. She didn't miss Charlie at all.

Each day she would write both the pros and cons of the three choices in a book. She struggled to make a decision based on her own idea of what was pro and what was con. Tessa continued to visit her mother while staying at Mrs. Racine's and she noticed that her mother was not as helpless as the family believed her to be. After the depression brought on by her mother's death, the year Tessa was ten, she had been seeing a therapist and a psychopharmacologist for anti-depressants. They had been working. Tessa realized her siblings were holding on to the old picture of their mother, as had Tessa until these last two weeks of non-judging observation. Her mother would be fine.

Tessa's two girl friends helped her search for more information on the Italian university and on the city of Venice, where it was located. Tessa then spoke to her professor about the option of deferring her acceptance.

A week later, Tessa was in the library researching resources for her mother and for further information on Venice. She started to laugh out loud. She realized that for the first time ever she felt comfortable in her own skin. She was conscious that she was feeling capable. Just as the use of the *NJSO Key* allowed her to observe her mother without old judgments, and to make room for the *Change-of-Perspective Key* on her keychain, she was now seeing herself in a more positive and capable light. She was aware that she was developing coping skills and her prison foundations were beginning to crack.

After two more weeks, Tessa went back home to the apartment she shared with Charlie. He said he was glad she'd come to her senses and that he had the information on apartments in Oakland, California, a city close to the job he was interviewing for. Tessa's immediate reaction was panic. Her heart was pounding, she was sweating and her legs felt weak. Charlie, not noticing Tessa's upset state, went on to say that Tessa would love Oakland and that he'd take care of them until Tessa could get a job and help out. He said he knew how hard decisions were for her, so he had done all of the research.

Tessa said she felt sick and went straight to bed. Charlie stormed out of the house. He was uneasy. He sensed that their pattern, of him making the decisions and Tessa willingly following, wasn't being played out.

In the quiet of the bedroom, Tessa's old Negative Self-Talk raged: "You're not good enough to live on your own!" it told her. Much to her surprise, another voice, one she was just starting to hear, began asking questions. The *Self-Questioning Key*, a precursor of many keys to follow, had become available to her in the two weeks she'd spent with Mrs. Racine. She was learning the value of this Key—the discovery of self. Tessa asked herself, as she felt her pulse slowing and her body relaxing, "Can I live with Charlie? Can I live with Charlie and be three thousand miles away from my mother now? *Do I want to*? Will my family think I'm selfish if I go to the university in Venice, even if I can defer the acceptance? Can I live in a foreign country by myself? *Do I want to*?" Tessa felt herself smile at her last question, "*Do I want to*?" She finally fell asleep with a head filled with unanswered questions.

In the morning, Tessa felt calm. This calm was unfamiliar to her because it was the calm that comes from being clear about what you want. Charlie was having coffee and looked up when Tessa walked into the kitchen. He said his interview was next week and he'd look at apartments while in California. Tessa took a breath and got ready to make the speech she had been practicing while brushing her teeth. It was a big risk for Tessa to talk to Charlie and tell him that she'd made an important decision, one that was based on her own needs. As soon as she'd woken up, she'd reviewed the little self-help book on healthy risk-taking that Mrs. Racine had left for her to read. It said that a healthy risk will have common elements:

1) It will be one YOU have decided is finally necessary to take.

2) You will know and feel that not taking it will keep you in a place you can no longer be.

3) You have decided taking the risk is less dangerous, mentally, physically and spiritually, than not taking it.

4) You will create optimal circumstances in which to use a Healthy-Risk Key. Optimal circumstances include the

location in which you feel most safe, a support system in place, and any additional information needed before you take action.

5) You will have full awareness of a possible worst-case scenario outcome, which needs to be considered before the Key is put in the lock.

Tessa said yes to all five statements and even made an early-morning call to her mother and sister Anita to have their support in place. With Keys in trembling hand, Tessa told Charlie she wasn't moving to California, that she was moving back to her mother's house. She said *she wanted* to help her mother with unfinished business connected to her father's death and *she wanted* to have some time with her mother before starting her graduate program in Italy. Charlie was actually speechless. Tessa felt as if a two-ton weight had been lifted off her shoulders.

Charlie's first words when he found his voice were, "You'll never be able to make it in a foreign country. You need me, Tessa." This stimulated Tessa's old internal **Negative Self-Talking Prisoner**, still fighting for its life. It was stirring up Tessa's lifelong doubts and her fears of inadequacy. The *Patience Key*, a new Key Tessa was cultivating, gave Tessa the moment she needed to not respond and to not do the old "I'm not okay" dance.

She exhaled and told Charlie, "It's a chance I have to take." The shiny *Success-in-Trying* and *Embrace-the-Unknown Keys* slipped onto her ever-growing chain.

Tessa spent the time before leaving for Italy helping her mother get her father's papers in order. She and her mother enjoyed quiet evenings together, sipping tea and planning the visit her mother and sister would make to Italy. Tessa's mother said she felt inspired by

Tessa's decision to do something so adventurous. Tessa would have her first school break in two months and would welcome the company of her family.

Tessa was hugging her mother goodbye when Mrs. Racine honked her car horn, signally that Tessa's ride to the airport had arrived. The bigger signal...Tessa had arrived. Tessa was free!

The Tessa Giovanni Story and Prison Break Model

Prisoner by:

Negative Self-Talk

> I'm not enough; I'm never going to…

Unhealthy Relationship Choice

> No. 4 You choose people who reinforce your Negative Self-Talk.

Goal Setting (The Setup)

> No. 1 You don't set a goal

> No. 2 You try to meet a goal someone else set for you.

Forts/Prisons:

> Too Nice

> Unhealthy Self-Judgment

> Avoidance of Pain

> Unhealthy Patterns

> Shame

Jailers:

> Peter Fog

> Maria Cant

> Kim Patterson

> Hugo First

Prison Break Keys:

> NJSO

> Self-Questioning

> Courage

> Healthy Risk

> Change-of-Perspective

> Success-in-Trying

> Embrace-the-Unknown

Prison Break Story No. 2: Mike Wilson

Mike is the protagonist in our second Prison Break story. You were introduced to Mike in Chapter Two, on Unhealthy Relationship Choices. We will follow Mike's unique path—from Mike the early Fort Builder, to Mike the proud Key Holder, who finds the Keys that will free him from thirty-five years of imprisonment.

Mike Wilson was born in a hospital on a military base in southern Texas. He was the first-born of Leonard and Debra Wilson. Mike's father, Leonard, came from a military family. In choosing a military career, Leonard was following in the footsteps of both his father and grandfather. Mike's mother Debra had played piano professionally, and was giving piano lessons from their home.

Leonard was a strict disciplinarian and didn't allow for "childish" behavior. He was always stressed because he was under the demanding eye of his decorated father, who was stationed on the same base. When Leonard was stressed, he would scream at Mike. Mike was only one and a half years old the first time this happened. Leonard had wanted Mike to be potty trained by now. Leonard was told that he had already been trained by this age. He didn't care that Mike's behavior in the area of potty training, and in other areas, was normal and age-appropriate. Mike's mother was the one who added balance to Mike's life with her more flexible nature and patience.

Unbeknownst to Mike, one of the three components of becoming a prisoner, **Negative Self-Talk, (the "I should")**, was now being planted in his wordless world, from the barrage of "You shoulds" thrown at him by his father.

When Mike was a child, he was in desperate need of a protective fort. He unconsciously built the **Fort of Perfection**, later to become his prison by the same name. At the time, building this fort was Mike's only means of survival. It made him safer to be a "perfect" child for his demanding father. His constant reach for perfection gave Mike a chance to experience his father's rare approval. Luckily Mike was very smart and an extremely hard worker. By the time his sister Anna was born, Mike was eight years old and excelled at everything. Mike was extremely busy with his school and after-school activities. These included the sports his father felt he "should" perfect and with the chores a boy his age "should" carry out. Mike's mother felt he was being pushed too hard, but she was preoccupied with her newborn child and was too tired to argue. Mike started to develop stomach problems and frequent headaches.

Sundays were Mike's only free time, since Saturday was a full-on chore day. Sunday was his favorite day. He and his mother would sit and play games when Anna was napping, or play duets on the piano, something Mike was naturally good at and truly enjoyed. However, it was the time with his father that made Sunday so special to him. When his father had the time, he would take Mike to hit golf balls, or for batting practice. Mike was nervous he wouldn't hit the golf ball well enough or the baseball far enough, but he was still glad for time with his father. Leonard was his most relaxed on the Sundays when he had no contact with Mike's grandfather. He was like a different person on those Sundays.

Years later, when Mike's father was ill and gave Mike an unexpected hug, it triggered a memory of a particular Sunday, when Mike was nine years old. He and his father had laughed so hard—a rare occurrence—because they realized that a golf ball Mike had hit (a ball they both thought must have gone far) was sitting at their feet, right on the tee. It had never been hit! That was one of the only times in his life that his father had given him a hug.

Throughout Mike's four years in high school, he kept up a frantic schedule. When Mike was a sophomore, he had an opportunity to try out as a piano player for the school band. His mother encouraged him, recognizing his innate ability, but Mike didn't believe he could excel at the piano even though he practiced. He didn't have time to practice enough, with time being consumed by the teams his father insisted he be on. Not being perfect wasn't an option. This early **Fort of Perfection** had become Mike's self-built **Prison of Perfection**.

Mike wasn't willing to try anything at which his success wasn't guaranteed. His unconscious self-talk was, "I'm going to be the best player or I don't play." This "all or nothing" stance made Mike a ready candidate for the **Prison of Rigidity**. Because Mike could only allow himself to participate in a sport at which he would excel, he became imprisoned by his method of goal-setting. Mike fell prey to **Goal Setting Setup No.4 (He set a goal, but couldn't focus on the process, he could only focus on the outcome.)**

Mike's, sister Anna, was eight years old when Mike was sixteen and in his third year of high school. Anna was petite and had thick chestnut hair and brown eyes practically the same color. Anna seemed to be the polar opposite of Mike. She was a relaxed, bubbly child. She was average in her schoolwork, and her only after-school activities were piano lessons. She had two close friends whom she talked to incessantly; she was a 'normal' pre-teen. Mike's father expected little of Anna and told her so on many occasions, in a piercingly loud voice. Mike was constantly trying to save Anna from this soul-hurting tirade and would tutor her to help raise her grades, or redo a chore that wasn't done "perfectly."

Mike, at sixteen, was already in the **Prison of Control**. He was vigilant about being in control of his life and Anna's and of his environment. This relentless control enabled him to be disciplined enough to achieve every goal and to continually save Anna from his father's verbal abuse. In his sixteenth year, Mike was hospitalized for a bleeding ulcer. The week following his operation was one of the happiest of his life. Mike's father was away on a training assignment in Germany. His mother and Anna took good care of him. His teams at school were able to put in temporary replacements and a good friend made sure he got all his assignments and notes. The house was filled with music, something his father didn't allow. Mike and his mother played the piano every day and Anna and her friends would listen, or at times gleefully sing to the music. For the first time that he could remember, Mike didn't feel rushed and yet he still got all his work done. He did things at a comfortable, yet unfamiliar pace. Mike didn't recognize that this was *his* pace, *his* rhythm.

Mike's goals, always strongly influenced by his father's expectations and demands, were that of a doer. Mike was unaware, at this time in his life, that his goal-setting style was a set up, because when setting goals, he didn't examine his nature and his personal rhythm. Mike was more a "be"-er than a doer. (**Goal Setting Setup No.5**). Mike's style of setting goals only deepened his prisoner status, established early on with his **Negative Self-Talk, "I Should."**

This week, with the *NJSO Key* in his hand for the first time, Mike observed that he was both a doer, and a "be"-er. The Prisoner was beginning to awaken, the Prison walls were showing a crack or two, and Mike was getting a fleeting whiff of what was to be a short-lived freedom.

When Mike's father returned the following week he was jubilant. He had secured their congressmen's endorsement, an endorsement that Mike would need to get into West Point. The congressman was coincidently in Germany at the same time as Mike's father, and they had long talks about Mike's qualifications for West Point.

Mike had applied to West Point at his father's "request," as well as applying to the schools he really wanted to attend. Mike's schools offered an excellent advanced computer science degree with a minor in music. When his father told him the "good news" Mike was speechless, which went unnoticed. Leonard was only focused on calling Mike's grandfather, hoping for some rare praise for his success in obtaining the congressman's endorsement of Mike.

Soon after his father's return, Mike's headaches started to increase in frequency and intensity. Because his jaw also hurt, he went to a dentist and was told that he was clenching his teeth and grinding them to the point of wearing down the enamel. Mike's unconscious **Prison of Anger** kept him locked inside himself, too afraid to speak up or to be aware of his own fury.

His unconscious Jailers were also working overtime. **Jason Wall,** threatened by Mike's recent realization that he was a doer and a "be"-er, was busy mortaring Mike's Prison walls. Consciousness is the Jailer's kryptonite. Jailer **I.E. Imagine** was also at work using her skill, creative negative thinking. She kept whispering softly to Mike how insane his father would be if Mike even considered not going to West Point. **Rosa Pinpointa,** Mike's third "Jailer Persona," was doing her share to instill in Mike a sense of optionlessness. As a result he began feeling that he had no choice!

Months later, when Mike was midway through his senior year, he received his acceptance to West Point. His father actually told Mike how proud he was that Mike was the first member of their military family to go to West Point. *Fait accompli.* Mike had the worst headache of his life and his mother insisted he have an MRI. She had a strong feeling the problem was not medical, but couldn't bring herself to talk to her husband.

Mike had started dating Lenore at the beginning of his senior year. She had encouraged him to take a risk and to tell his father that he didn't want to go to West Point and that he didn't want a career in the military. Lenore didn't know Mike's father. She didn't understand the immense courage Mike would need to say this. When Mike, in utter desperation, did think about telling his father, he was sure that the worst-case scenario would occur: that his father would disown him, or at the very least, never speak to him again.

These thoughts showed that Mike had the **Healthy-Risk Key** within his reach, as well as the **Self-Questioning Key**. He had consciously decided it was too great a risk. Mike was desperately in need of two Keys he didn't yet possess, the **Courage Key** and the **Embrace-the-Unknown Key**. The MRI showed no medical problem related to the brain as a cause of Mike's headache.

Fast-forward to Mike's first year at West Point. He did well enough, despite continued stomach problems, frequent headaches and lack of sleep. His father told Mike that his grades had to be better. His father said this while looking into the face of his pale, bleary-eyed son. Finally, his mother stepped in and said, "Enough!"

All hell broke loose. At the end of his freshman year and to the horror and shame of his grandfather and father, Mike left West Point. Mike's father couldn't forgive him. He told Mike he was a failure and an embarrassment to the family. He would scream at Mike for the littlest thing and the atmosphere in the house over the summer became unbearable. At the end of August, Mike's father came home on a rampage after he ran into the congressman who had endorsed Mike. All day long he screamed at Mike, "You dishonored me, you dishonored me." His tirade got so loud and frightening that Anna locked herself in her room and refused to open the door. No one was able to get Leonard to control his behavior; that night Mike, his mother, and his sister Anna moved out. They moved into an apartment and tried to put themselves back together again. They now had to make plans for an uncertain future.

Mike spoke to the college he had most wanted to attend when he had been forced by his father to accept West Point's offer. After hearing his story, the college said they would accept him for the February semester, contingent upon his agreement to go to counseling with their school psychologist.

Mike's mother decided to see the Army chaplain for guidance. She knew and respected him and Anna was still in a teen group he was facilitating. Mike's father, out of respect for the chaplain and not to appear uncooperative, agreed to go to one marriage counseling session.

By the time Mike graduated from college, he was engaged to Lenore, his high school sweetheart. His parents had been reunited after completing two years of work with the chaplain, and when finished, continuing to work on their marriage on their own. Mike's grandfather, to everybody's surprise, was the greatest supporter of the reconciliation. He finally admitted that his only regret was the end of his marriage to Mike's grandmother. Anna was sixteen and was balancing college applications and an active social life.

The company Mike worked for in the summers of his freshman, sophomore and junior years, as well as two other companies, had offered Mike a full-time opportunity as a computer programmer. He took the job that he was most familiar with, that company he had worked for during the three summers he was in college.

Over the year, Mike frequently questioned his choice of this job. He had that *Self-Questioning Key* firmly in his pocket, but he was unclear about the answers. Mike was into the twelfth year of his job, and the eleventh year of his marriage to Lenore, when his headaches again became more frequent and more forceful. Both he and Lenore were aware that these headaches were most probably emotional.

Mike was about to become aware of something else. He had unconsciously made an unhealthy relationship choice many years ago and its full effect was now causing him great pain. Mike made **Unhealthy Relationship Choice No. 1: He chose someone with the negative personality traits of the parent he needed to fix.**

Mike had a good marriage. Lenore *was not* Mike's Unhealthy Relationship Choice. If he had married any parent by choosing Lenore, it was his mother. He and Lenore loved each other and they had developed a healthy communication system, which, for the most part, nipped their problems in the bud. Talking at dinner about the intensity of Mike's headaches and exploring possible reasons for the increased severity, Mike told Lenore he had been asking himself the same questions. At the end of the evening Mike and Lenore were in agreement about the source.

The following day, Mike's Unhealthy Relationship Choice No. 2 was his relationship with Bill, his boss at work. Mike decided to take a risk, and use the *Healthy-Risk Key*, to free himself and speak to some co-workers about their experience of Bill.

Sometimes, workplaces are unconsciously chosen to replicate your family of origin. You unknowingly make this familiar choice in order to have a second chance to fix what or who you couldn't fix in that original family system. (Do you remember these next few paragraphs from Mike's earlier vignette?) Mike worked for a computer software firm and was in a department that consisted of only eight people. Bill, the manager, was smart, arrogant and verbally abusive. He treated everyone abusively. Mike and his co-workers were overachievers. They worked hard and the department did well. Mike had the same stomach problem and painful headaches he'd had as a child and is frequently absent due to illness. He missed several staff meetings. Bill always picked on someone at staff meetings. At one meeting, Mike summoned the courage to stand up to Bill, who was mercilessly berating Betty, the youngest team member. Betty resembled Mike's younger sister. Bill punished Mike for standing up to him, overloading him with parts of the job Mike found most distasteful. Ernesto, another member of Mike's work family, quit after complaining for a year about the manager's verbally abusive behavior. Three months later, much to everybody's surprise, he returned to his former position, leaving a job where the department head was easy going.

One day, when Bill was away, and the group was having lunch together, Mike told everybody that Ernesto's return made him think about why he stayed in such a tense work situation. He asked the group a personal question, "How many of you had a verbally abusive parent?" After a moment of silence, all six of Mike's co-workers raised their hands. Ernesto blurted out, "I couldn't help myself. I was drawn to come back."

That night at dinner, Mike told Lenore he realized that he had hoped that if he worked really hard and did well for the team, Bill would appreciate him and be nicer to him. This is just what he had always sort from his father. "No more moth to the flame for me," Mike told Lenore. They discussed Mike's options (**Optimize-Options Key**) before turning out the lights.

Mike had a plan. Lenore had left a pad on the kitchen table; the first empty page was titled "Mike's imperfect plan!!!" He smiled as he used the pad to list the companies that had offered him jobs twelve years ago, and he made a list of others in his field that he knew were hiring. He found the phone numbers and names of each contact person. Next to his coffee cup were two Keys. One he had used just last night, the *Optimize-Options Key*, which helped him widen his focus so he and Lenore could brainstorm other avenues of employment. Jailer **Rosa Pinpointa** was quaking.

The other Key waiting to be noticed was the *Think-Out-Of-The-Box Key*. Use of this Key enabled Mike to consider something his previous narrow focus and his imprisonment in the **Prison of Anger** would never have let him consider. He decided to connect with his network of Army personnel to see if anyone was in need of his computer skills. Mike's education, experience, and first-hand knowledge of the workings of the military would make him a viable candidate for such a position.

The first step, and to Mike the most terrifying, that he and Lenore had discussed, was to speak privately with Bill about his abusive style and Mike's inability to stay at his job unless it changed. Mike knew he was at a no-choice point. His health, both physical and mental, was now on the line.

Mike hadn't had the courage as a child or teenager to speak up to his father. He didn't have the keys or support he needed to take such a frightening action. His Prisons and Jailers kept him unhealthily protected from pain. As an adult, he consciously knew that he couldn't fix or change his father and probably couldn't fix or change Bill, but he now had the Keys and the support he needed to be able to tell Bill what he would no longer tolerate.

Mike had just shattered the walls of his old and protective fort and his present Prison, the **Prison of Avoidance of Pain**. Mike came to realize the truth of the saying, "There is no greater pain than the pain of avoiding pain."

When Mike walked into work, you could hear him jingling all the way down the hallway, his keychain full. On it he carried the **Courage Key, Healthy-Risk Key, Optimize-Options Key, Think Out-Of-The-Box Key, Success-in-Trying Key** and **Self-Esteem Key**, the noisiest of all.

No matter how his talk with Bill turned out, Mike was free!

The Mike Wilson Story and Prison Break Model

Prisoner by:

Negative self-Talk

    I should

Unhealthy Relationship Choice

    No.1 You choose someone with the negative personality traits of the parent you wanted to fix.

Goal-setting (The Setup)

    No.4 You set a goal and don't focus on the process-—you only focus on the outcome. You give yourself no credit for embarking on the journey.

    No.5 You don't examine your nature, and personal rhythm. Are you more a doer or a "be"-er?

Forts/Prisons:

    Perfection

    Rigidity-—All or Nothing

    Control

    Anger

    Avoidance of Pain

Jailers:

    Jason Wall

    I.E Imagine

    Rosa Pinpointa

Prison Break Keys:

| NJSO | Optimize-Options | Think-Out-of-The Box |
| Self-Questioning | Success-in-Trying | |

Courage   Embrace-the-Unknown

Healthy-Risk   Self-Acceptance

Prison Break Story No. 3: Suki Takahashi

Suki Takahashi is an only child. She was born three years after her parents, both in their mid-thirties at the time, immigrated from Tokyo to the United States. The family was hard-working and saved money to send to Japan, to help more of their family immigrate to the United States.

Suki's mother was a fine cook. She believed Suki was too thin and she tried to fatten her up, primarily for her health, but also as a symbol of prosperity. A round, well-fed child reflected well on a family. Her mother's cooking produced a healthier, but heavier Suki. She wasn't fat by any means, but in comparison to her nuclear and extended family Suki was the heaviest and tallest. These physical differences were only outward manifestations of her internal sense of being different. She never felt as though she fit in anywhere.

Suki was caught between the traditions of her Japanese home life and the traditions of the United States, her country of birth. In traditional Japanese homes, the father works and the mother takes care of home and child. A meal is always waiting for the returning father and eaten at the same time each day. Suki's parents faithfully followed the tradition of removing their shoes and placing them in an area between the front door and main living area, the "genkan no ma," and pointing the shoes outwards, showing an intention to leave, a tradition called "dosoku genkin." Suki was totally embarrassed by these traditions and feared being laughed at by visiting friends. Despite the fact that many Americans prefer shoes be left at the door to keep dirt out, few would ask a family member or guest to rotate the shoes to point outward. Suki, having developed few coping skills by the age of ten, handled her self-consciousness about her weight and her height, and her embarrassment over her parent's accent and their traditions, by becoming a loner.

To handle the internal confusion caused by being caught between two cultures, Suki built the Fort of Rigidity. This childhood fort morphed into the **Prison of Rigidity.** In Suki's early adult life this prison kept her from all of life's grey areas because this is a prison of all or nothing, black or white.From an early age, Suki's **Negative Self-Talk, ("I'm Not Good Enough," "I Should")** was, "I'm too tall. I'm too fat. I should be like the other kids in my class." This early negative monologue was an unconscious foundation for Suki's later conscious monologue, "I'm not good enough. I should be thinner, faster, friendlier."

At parent-teacher conferences, Suki's parents were told that she was an average student and very well behaved, but that she didn't interact with the other students, and never voluntarily spoke up in class. The only team she tried out for was the cross-country team, the least interactive sport offered. Suki's parents knew that running was something Suki did to lose weight. She ran three miles every day after school, and this rain-or-shine discipline, for a twelve-year-old, concerned them. Suki was losing weight. The problem was that she was losing too much weight. She hadn't been overweight in the first place. This problem was given a name by their family doctor two years later…anorexia.

Fourteen-year-old Suki and her parents, at their appointment with Dr. Hall, a specialist in eating disorders, were told that anorexia was a problem of control, and was often about family enmeshment, not food. During their fifth therapy session, Suki's parents said that they realized they had been too protective of Suki because she was their only child and because they themselves had fears as foreigners in a new country. They saw, in talking to Dr. Hall, that they weren't only afraid for Suki's safety, but also for their own. Suki's mother remembered that for the first five or six years she was in this country, she was always afraid. Being home alone with Suki kept them both cocooned in a familiar and insulated world. The world outside her door, so very unfamiliar, had terrified Suki's mother. "I had forgotten how bad those first five or six years were," she said, clutching her husband's hand. Despite her fear, she said that she thought she had encouraged Suki to have friends, to go to parties, and to invite friends over.

In that same session, a sullen Suki said that she stayed home because she would rather read her stamp catalogues and run her three miles than go to parties. She only had one friend and she wasn't invited to parties. Months later, when Suki was working alone with Dr. Hall, and her parents were only called when needed, she was able to admit that she often felt worried about leaving her mother alone. Maybe, Dr. Hall interjected, Suki was still reacting to memories of a mother who was always fearful. Suki also admitted that she felt guilty about her embarrassment over the foreignness of her parents' traditions. Suki's **Prisons of Guilt and Worry** had her firmly incarcerated. She was often kept in solitary confinement.

Suki was just starting to become conscious of the reasons she felt guilty and the reasons she often worried, but she wasn't ready to feel the initial pain that can accompany this awareness. Suki wasn't ready for the pain of letting her walls down. This non-readiness activated one of Suki's vigilant Jailers, **Jason Wall.** To bring her back to a "painless" unconsciousness, he started to fill the cracks in her Prison wall caused by her momentary insight. Dr. Hall suggested that she talk to her parents about this guilt and worry, or they could have a joint session.

Suki's walls were weakening and before she was able to hold the *Courage Key* in her hand and speak to her parents, she got back into her **Prison of Control** and locked herself in. Jailers **Peter Fogg** and **Maria Cant** stood guard. Soon, Suki began to feel desperate. She needed to run to feel in control again, and she needed to run to lose some weight. To her they were one and the same. Suki had cut out her daily three-mile run until her weight increased, an agreement she'd made with her parents. She felt great pressure to stick to the agreement. Suki didn't see that this agreement, this goal, was really another prisoner-making component. Without realizing it, Suki set **Goal Setup No. 3: a goal with unrealistic expectations for who you are at the time of setting.** Suki really wasn't able, at this moment in her life, to completely give up running. The rigidity that had protected her as a child was now confining her to an untenable position. Her **Prison of Rigidity** made no room for revisions. Suki was imprisoned by the belief that she either ran her three miles or didn't run at all. This rigidity kept her from entertaining the option of running a shorter distance. "Partial" was a forbidden word in her Prison system.

In Suki's frenzy to avoid the pain of being so out of control, she unconsciously built yet another prison, the **Prison of Avoidance of Pain.** She started to run again and nervously hid it from her parents. The ensuing weight loss, exhaustion, and bitter winter weather caused Suki to be sick most of the winter and early spring. When she was getting her strength back and had regained the eight pounds she had lost, she decided to start a more reasonable exercise program of walking one- and-a-half-miles a day. Although this was a great breakthrough for Suki, it was still a *setup*. It was a goal that wasn't possible for her to achieve at this time in her weakened condition.

The way Suki went about her modified goal to walk only one-and-a-half miles a day was another setup. She continued to work with Dr. Hall, but despite his support of Suki's attempts to make modifications, she couldn't give herself credit for embarking on the journey. She was too weak and out of shape to walk her new goal of one-and-a-half miles in the hot August weather. The first day, Suki made a half-mile with great difficulty. She forgot to bring water, and she started at a pace she used to jog at but now wasn't ready to sustain. That night her Negative Self-Talk was running wild; the "not good enough" and the "I should" bounced off the walls. Suki never recognized that the half-mile she walked was farther than she had walked since her recovery from illness. Determined to meet the mile-and-a-half goal the next day, she got up at 6:00am to beat the heat, carried a water bottle, and went a tad slower.

Suki made three-quarters of a mile with the aid of these modifications. A healthy goal-setter would have felt good that there was improvement. The process was in place and working. Suki, being a Prisoner of **Goal Setup No.4 who focused on the outcome, rather than the process**, was mortified that she had made these changes and not succeeded. She felt disabled. She couldn't bear to try again because it was too devastating that she couldn't meet such an easy goal.

Despite the praise of her family, friends, and her doctor for being able to do three-quarters of a mile under such conditions, Suki abandoned her goal and stopped going to therapy. Suki was at a low point in her young life. She was just barely able to graduate from high school. She didn't know what to do next.

The next five years were like a never-ending roller coaster ride. Suki's anorexia, her only means of controlling her life, had returned with a vengeance. When she was in therapy with Dr. Hall she had started to develop other coping skills to handle the pain of feeling out of control. When Suki was twenty-three she was still living at home. She was running in snow, sleet and rain, and she was doing nothing else. Her parents could no longer stand by and watch her go downhill. They insisted that she return to therapy or they'd have her hospitalized.

Suki resumed her therapy with Dr. Hall. When Suki was in her fifth year of therapy, she was no longer engaged in anorexic behaviors. Suki and her father shared a passion for stamp collecting. He suggested that she apprentice with his friend Tim who owned the 'The Stamp Sampler,' a shop Suki and her father had often visited. Tim had also immigrated with his family from Japan. He and Suki's father met at a philatelic club shortly after Suki was born.

Suki was twenty-eight when she walked into Tim's shop again. It was the first time in her life that she felt as though she fit in. Suki apprenticed to Tim and then became a full-time employee. Over the seven years she worked for him, she got the experience as well as the knowledge that would qualify her to become a stamp appraiser. Tim's apartment was above the shop and every day at teatime Suki would go upstairs, put her shoes in the hallway pointing outward, following the dosoku genkin tradition. She was beginning to own these traditions, and she had no shame attached to that awareness. Now, Suki was also the proud Key holder of the **NJSO Key, Change-of -Perspective Key** and the glorious **Self-Acceptance Key**.

Suki's blossoming awareness was facilitated by her relationship with Hideaki, Tim's nephew. Hideaki had worked with his uncle since he was a young boy. He was already, at the age of thirty-six, a respected rare stamp dealer. Suki's respect for him as a person who practiced and valued the traditions of his heritage, and as a respected professional, made it easier for her to accept her own parents' traditions. It made it possible for Suki to ultimately accept herself as a willing practitioner of Japanese traditional life.

This emerging freedom was a result of Suki's courage to see that she valued her family traditions. She was able to see that she was a loner by nature, not just by defense, and to embrace that aspect of herself. During the seven years she worked for Tim, Suki used the *NJSO Key*. She kept it in her pocket at all times, along with the *Self-Questioning Key* and the *Courage Key*. This was the beginning of her well-earned Prison Break.Hideaki asked Suki if she wanted to go into business with him, to start their own shop with the help and blessing of his Uncle Tim. He told Suki that their talents complemented each other. Suki had the eye to identify a rare stamp on sight and had accumulated a vast knowledge of the history of stamp production. With a trained eye, she had the focus that was needed to stay on top of a changing market that determined a rare stamp's value. Hideaki also had, he said, the necessary knowledge and experience for success in the endeavor he was proposing. The piece he had, that Suki was missing, was that he was naturally comfortable with small talk and networking with potential buyers. Interacting with customers was essential at the trade shows they would have to attend. Suki's old prisoner-making component, the Negative Self-Talk was now silent. Suki knew she wasn't a social person and, miraculously, that felt fine. Acknowledging that she possessed the needed skills Hideaki highlighted, she was grateful for her natural and worked-for abilities. Actually, over the last few years, the *Gratefulness Key* frequented her keychain.

Suki was willing to take the risk of going into business with Hideaki because she had asked herself the five Healthy-Risk Questions and answered yes to all five.

1) Will the risk be one I have decided is finally necessary to take?

2) Will I know and feel that not taking it will keep me in a place I can no longer be?

3) Will I have decided taking the risk is less dangerous, mentally, physically and spiritually, then not taking it?

4) Can I create optimal circumstances in which to use the **Healthy Risk-Key**? (Optimal circumstances include a location in which you feel most safe, a support system in place, and any additional information needed before you take action.)

5) Am I fully aware of a possible worst-case scenario outcome, which needs to be considered before the key is put in the lock?

Suki added the **Healthy-Risk Key** to her ever-growing key-chain and was about to become a frequent user of the **Success-in-Trying Key** over the thirty-five years she and Hideaki would own their stamp shop.

Three years into their business partnership, Suki and Hideaki became more than business partners. Suki *did not* make an unhealthy relationship choice by accepting his proposal. Suki told Hideaki, when he proposed, that she wanted a combined Japanese and Western wedding. She wanted to be married by a Shinto priest in Shinto style at a shrine. Suki wanted a ceremony in which she and Hideaki were purified, drank sake, and where the groom read the words of commitment. To follow the tradition of giving a symbolic offering to Kami at the end of the ceremony was important to her. The Western traditions she hoped he would agree to were to have the shrine set up inside a hotel, to wear western clothes rather than kimonos, and to make the speech at the end of the party to all their guests, a Japanese tradition usually performed by both bride and groom.

This outward coming together of Eastern and Western traditions in her wedding celebration reflected the years of work Suki had consciously done to blend and accept these divergent aspects of herself. As Suki walked down the aisle, her parents on either side, she heard the melodic tinkling music of her Keys. The loudest of all was the **Gratefulness Key**. Suki was free!

The Suki Takahashi Story and Prison Break Model

Prisoner by:

> *Negative self-Talk*
>
> I'm not enough
>
> I should

Goal Setting Setup

No.3 You set a goal that is unrealistic to accomplish, for the person you are, at the time of setting. Of course these are not unrealistic goals if you are Mother Theresa, the Bionic Man, or Hercules.

No.4 You set a goal and don't focus on the process. You only focus on the out come. You give yourself no credit for embarking on the journey.

Forts/Prisons:

> Rigidity Unhealthy Self-Judgment
>
> Guilt and Worry
>
> Shame
>
> Avoidance of Pain
>
> Control

Jailers:

> Peter Fog
>
> Maria Cant
>
> Jason Wall

Prison Break Keys:

NJSO	Change-of-Perspective
Self-Questioning	Success-in-Trying
Courage	Gratefulness
Healthy-Risk	Self-Acceptance

Prison Break Story No. 4: Devon Sims

You were first introduced to Devon Sims in Chapter Two, on Unhealthy Relationship Choices. Here we will follow him on the path that led him to make his unhealthy choices, and then continue to follow him while he wends his way to freedom from all the Prisons he built along the way.

Devon Sims was born in Pine Bush, a small town in upstate New York. His father, Curtiss, was a Park Ranger in the Minnewaska Park Preserve, which was only a twenty-minute drive from their home. His mother, Mae, stayed at home raising the children. Devon, the oldest of five, was the only child for the first four years of his life. These were the years when he formed a strong and loving bond with his mother. He adored her. When Devon was four, his brother Vern was born. Two years later, Lionel was born; two years after that, Tyrone; and three years later, the last child and the only girl, Kitty, was born. His parents had a very good relationship.

Devon loved nature. He hiked, went fishing, and loved to take walks in the quiet hardwood forests of the Shawangunk Mountain Ridge. He had two good friends. One, his friend Eric, lived on a nearby dairy farm. For Devon's thirteenth birthday, Eric gave Devon and their other friend Pat hooded sweatshirts with the saying, *Butter Capital of the World* silk-screened across the back. Devon had five of these. Each year, Eric gave him one of the unsold sweatshirts from his father's booth at the annual County Fair.

When Devon was only fifteen-years-old, a tragedy occurred. Unbeknownst to Devon, it was the year several of his future Prisons went into construction. Devon's mother was killed in a terrible car accident. Each member of the family had their own way of handling this tragedy. Devon's father buried himself in work and stayed away from his family, who continually triggered his intense pain. His father's reaction created problems because the children needed care. They were only fifteen, eleven, nine, seven and four at the time of Mae's death. Devon unconsciously became the default father, the diffuser of differences, and the "good" responsible child. This is when he built the **Prison of Too Nice,** where he was to remain incarcerated for decades.

Since Devon was the oldest child and his father was in hiding from his own pain, Devon took on responsibilities too great for a fifteen-year-old to handle. He now set goals that made him an unconscious Prisoner, especially of **Goal Setting Setup No.3 -You set a goal with unrealistic expectations for who you are at the time of setting.** It was impossible for even the most responsible fifteen-year-old to handle the burden so suddenly thrust upon Devon. Sadly, he had no time to mourn his loss of a beloved mother, and his feelings went quickly underground. These feelings, the reasons for his future choices, were only beginning to become available to Devon again when he was in his thirties. This made many of his own choices between the ages of fifteen and his mid-thirties a mystery to him.

Devon believed that he was honoring his mother by taking care of her children. He became the calm in their storm. He, on the other hand, had no one to calm and nurture him. He was busy building Prisons, from his childhood forts. Devon had little need of protective forts before his mother's death. The child-rearing mistakes, becoming mother and father to four children when he was so young, made him a Prisoner of the complex **Prison of Guilt and Worry.** He lived within its walls on an almost daily basis.

Devon's salvation was his solitary hikes in the forest and his occasional fishing trips in the nearby lakes. Ralph and Lorna, Devon's maternal uncle and his wife, helped with the children as much as possible to give Devon time for his own schoolwork and his two stress-reducing activities.

Devon mentioned to his father that he was looking for a job to start as soon as he graduated from high school that June. Devon's dream job was to be a fishing guide in Alaska. He knew that wasn't possible in the present situation and the responsibility he felt for his siblings, but he still hoped to find an outdoor job. This was a realistic goal, since they lived so close to several large natural preserves, and with the contacts his father had as a Park Ranger.

His father, without consulting Devon or honoring Devon's need of an outdoor job, asked Devon's Uncle Ralph if he could give Devon a job in his cabinetry shop. He needed Devon to remain close to home and have the flexibility to take care of the children. He told Ralph that Devon was very handy, that he had a natural love of wood, and that he was a very hard and dependable worker. Ralph, knowing Devon well, needed little convincing. He called Devon the next day to offer him a job starting in September. Devon quickly accepted, not realizing that his father was instrumental in this offer. He was unconsciously following a goal set by another, this was **Goal-Setting Setup No. 2 -You try to meet a goal someone else set for you**, and it deepened Devon's Prisoner status. Devon started his new job, took care of the children and fit in a hike whenever his father was home or his aunt and uncle had the kids over.

Ralph's wife, Lorna, was worried that Devon never had time to go out with his friends or go on a date like other kids his age. Devon was nineteen and had only gone on a handful of dates in his senior year of high school. Lorna decided to introduce him to her friend's daughter, Yvonne, who worked in the hospital where Lorna was a nurse. Yvonne was a lovely young woman who lived in the town of New Paltz, not far from Pine Bush. She loved to hike, to walk in the Preserve on her birding walks, and to canoe on the Shawangunk Kill. Devon and Yvonne dated for six years. Yvonne was ready to be married, but Devon, unconscious of his imprisonment in the **Prison of Avoidance of Pain**, couldn't bring himself to make the commitment. He loved Yvonne. He loved her very much. The more he cared about her the more distant he became. Devon couldn't understand his own distancing. He wasn't yet in touch with the awareness that this distancing was his fifteen-year-old's fort of protection, created when his mother suddenly died. This fort was built in response to Devon's unconscious promise to himself, "I'll never let myself love anybody so much again. I can't ever feel pain like this again." By the time he was twenty-five the fort had become a thick-walled prison and all three of Devon's Jailers, **Hugo First, I.E. Imagine,** and **Jason Wall**, made sure Devon stayed safely imprisoned.

When Yvonne broke up with Devon he was sad, or he thought, "I should feel sad," but his stronger feeling was one of relief. Devon's family, who loved Yvonne, couldn't understand Devon's lack of reaction and his ability to put his relationship behind him so quickly. Devon didn't understand his own reactions. He asked himself, "Did I really love her? Can I love anyone?" The *Self-Questioning Key* was available and waiting, but Devon stopped at those two questions. He wasn't ready to open his Pandora's Box.

Instead, this was a time of active Prison building. Devon had unconsciously built a new prison, and it continued the protection of an old fort by keeping him from examining his hidden painful feelings around the loss of someone he loved. This new Prison had the additional benefit of keeping Devon from checking out his dream of being a fishing guide in Alaska. The **Prison of Fear of the Unknown** is densely populated with many prisoners who are known, in the prison system, as lifers.Five years after Yvonne left him, he met

Trisha. Before Trisha, he hadn't dated anyone for more than four months. He met Trisha while visiting Mohonk Mountain House with his father and his four siblings for Mohonk's famous Sunday Brunch. This was arranged and paid for by his father in celebration of Devon's thirtieth birthday.

Devon was now an established cabinet-maker and his uncle had just made him a partner in his business. Devon was good at managing his money and always lived within his means. He finally had a chance to put some money away for the future. Devon's siblings were now twenty-six, twenty-four, twenty-two, and nineteen. Two of his brothers, Vern and Lionel, had joined the Marines and were home on leave from overseas. The twenty-two-year old, Tyrone, had graduated with a degree in forestry. Devon's sister Kitty was in her second year at a local community college. Devon still felt responsibility for them, but now this responsibility was finally shared with his father, who was no longer running away from the pain of a loss that had happened fifteen years ago.

Devon was with Trisha for four years. Again, the **Unhealthy Pattern** repeated. Trisha was ready to get married, they were very compatible, and again Devon's family really liked her. Devon did his old dance, his unconscious mind telling him, "You love this woman, you could get very hurt. Move back, save yourself." When Trisha left Devon, he told himself he wasn't going to get seriously involved again.

For the next six years, Devon lived a simple life in his own home in Pine Bush. He made a decent living and was taking over more of the responsibilities as Ralph headed toward retirement. His sister and brothers all remained on the East Coast, no further than an eight-hour drive.

Devon's father had died six months ago. Devon, at forty, was starting to feel lonely and have yearnings for a family of his own. This frightened him. He started to ask himself why he was so afraid. Devon had always had courage, but now he used his **Courage Key** to continue to question himself and to hear the answers. He was starting to discover, through his own honest self-questioning, that his fear and loneliness was connected to the unbearable pain he still remembered when he lost his mother. He was finally making connections and realized that he would rather be alone than ever feel that pain again. Could he use the **Healthy-Risk Key**, as well as the **Courage Key** he had on his keychain? Could he now hear the answers to his own questions? Could Devon risk meeting someone and loving her fully? The keys were near at hand; the prison doors were opening. In walked Fiona.

Because of his loneliness, Devon agreed to go with his friend Eric to a party a mutual friend was throwing for his wife's fortieth birthday in Manhattan. Eric had left his family's dairy farm fifteen years before and moved to Manhattan. He worked at any jobs he could while following his passion for acting. Marta, the birthday girl, had a part in the same play in which Eric had a substantial lead role. Devon rarely went to Manhattan. The noise, the crowds, and the quality of air were opposite from the environment that Devon was comfortable in. At Eric's insistence, he went to the party. (The next several paragraphs might sound familiar. They are from Devon's earlier vignette.) When Fiona walked in the door, Devon actually felt himself being pulled in her direction. She was pulsing with energy from her 5'8" frame. Her clothes were floating around her, Devon thought, and her laugh was infectious as she greeted Eric, who was heading toward her. Devon talked to her briefly, and though she wandered off to talk with other guests, Devon stayed infused with her energy. She was nothing like Trisha or his first love, Yvonne although he was sure she had forgotten him the minute she left their conversation, but Devon's thoughts of her lingered all week. He'd never met anyone like her before, but having met her, his loneliness intensified.

Surprisingly, Eric called at the end of the week to say that Fiona had asked a lot of questions about him and hinted she would like it if he called. Devon made that first call, and the next year was a whirlwind. Devon and Fiona had an intense physical chemistry that made up for their incompatibility in other areas. At first Devon was flattered that Fiona wanted him to spend all their alone time at her place in the city. "Your house is a bit small," she said, with her alluring smile. He missed his alone time in his home but wanted to be with her. He went to more parties in this one year than in his entire life. He couldn't wait to leave, but still enjoyed watching Fiona "flow" around the room. Devon and Fiona valued fitness, and worked out together, which was a positive way to spend time together. Fiona said she liked Devon's family. They didn't like her and kept this to themselves. They were so glad that he was dating again and seemed less lonely. They had reservations because of Fiona's flamboyant appearance and her lifestyle, which was so different from Devon's preferred style. One of Devon's and Fiona's big differences started to undermine that initial magnetic pull. It was their very different attitudes toward handling money.

Both Devon and Fiona did well financially. Devon was not a spender, But Fiona was. Devon, though he had no children, looked ahead and was saving for college educations he might one day need to pay for. He wanted to be able to help his brothers and sister, his nieces and nephews if need be. Fiona had no children and she lived in the moment. "Why save for something that might never happen," she often said to Devon. "Why deprive myself of the life my hard-earned money affords me?"

Devon realized his spending had doubled in the time Fiona had been in his life. He reluctantly agreed to go on a very expensive vacation, traveling first class, staying at five-star hotels and going on expensive tours and to even more expensive nightclubs. They argued at each juncture. Fiona won each time, but Devon withdrew more and more and got angrier and angrier with himself for not saying no to what he considered excess.

Their differences were, for the most part, balanced by an intense sexual chemistry. But even this was affected by Devon's discomfort with the extravagant gifts Fiona lavished on his nieces and nephews.

At the end of their first year as a couple, Fiona felt they should buy a house together. Devon's place was so small, she now said, without her alluring smile. It was time to live together, she insisted, over and over again. Devon was still drawn to Fiona's energy, an energy he didn't have and that he admired. He was also drawn to the sexual intimacy they shared. This intimacy was far less frightening than other forms of intimacy he'd with Yvonne and Trisha. The strong pull he felt toward Fiona wasn't enough for him to give up his home in Pine Bush, but he agreed to share a rental for a year. Fiona picked apartments more expensive than Devon would consider, although with their combined incomes they could afford this high price range. Fiona started showing Devon apartments in busy mid-town Manhattan, close to the theater district where she was presently working. In a fearful moment when Fiona hinted that the relationship would be over unless Devon agreed to this eighteen-hundred-square foot-apartment in the heart of the city, he acquiesced.

On a Saturday morning, Devon sat in their beautifully decorated apartment, in the very noisy heart of this big city, far from lakes and woods. He had to commute back and forth to his business in Pine Bush every day. As each day passed, the feeling that he was a prisoner grew. In fact Devon was a prisoner of the Unhealthy Relationship that is formed when you choose someone <u>so</u> different from you.

Devon became susceptible to every cold and flu he was exposed to. His immune system was depressed from the stress of his daily commute and the tension of a city environment. His shrinking savings were another stress on his mind and body and he began his pattern of withdrawal. This withdrawal was not triggered by an unconscious fear of love and loss, but rather by not wanting to be where he was and feeling unable to extricate himself. Devon's Jailers were keeping him locked in the **Prison of Too Nice**, and he was paying the high price for the "safety" of incarceration. Now it was time for Devon's siblings to take care of him. They painfully watched Devon shrink into himself and noticed many new lines on his handsome face. This was a man they loved and so they decided to take action. Vern called a family meeting. They made a plan to confront Devon. They wanted to tell him how they saw Fiona and his relationship with her. Tyrone felt polar opposites weren't a strong enough description for Devon and Fiona. Actually, Devon had made the **Unhealthy Relationship Choice No.5 (You choose someone <u>so</u> different from you)**.

The intervention was held at the home of Kitty, who was now married with two children. The siblings were shaken when Devon cried. They had never seen him cry. They described what he meant to them and their pain at seeing him living so ungenuinely. He seemed like a wounded, caged animal. By the end of the evening they were laughing as they ate Kitty's ribs, collard greens and black-eyed peas. This was the dish their mother Mae was famous for.

Devon told Fiona the very next day that he would pay his share of the rent until the termination of the lease at the end of the year, but he was leaving before its expiration. This assurance that he would pay his half of this very high rent until the lease terminated softened Fiona's reaction. She took the news with little emotion.

When Devon was resettled in his Pine Bush log cabin home, he felt a flood of gratefulness. This was the same feeling he'd had when his siblings had expressed their love and appreciation for him. The *Gratefulness Key* was his.

Devon devoted the following year to himself. His time was spent asking himself the questions he'd been too afraid to ask years ago, and they were leading him to truthful answers. He was now aware that he had chosen Fiona, and to a degree committed to her, because he didn't love her. If he lost Fiona, the pain wouldn't be great, as it would have been if he had committed to Yvonne or Trisha and had lost either of them. This was especially true of Yvonne, whom he now realized he had loved very much. It took courage to see the truth of this unhealthy pattern, the reasons for his prison construct. With the *Courage Key* on his chain, and *Healthy-Risk Key* beckoning, Devon was finally walking out of two of his prisons; the **Prison of Too Nice**, and the **Prison of Avoidance of Pain**. He was no longer willing to pay the high price of unconsciousness.

He was patient, and he was determined not to date until he cleared up his own confusion and was able to make conscious what he had for so long tried to keep unknown.

During this year of conscious growth, Devon's keychain became full. He used all his Keys: the *NJSO Key* to observe himself safely; the *Courage Key* to allow him to make this observation; the *Self-Questioning Key* so that he could connect to his true self, the self he was before his mother's death; the *Self-Trust Key*, so that his remembrance of who he genuinely was could be trusted to be the truth. And finally, he used the *Self-Acceptance Key*, which freed him to be himself, limitations and all.

Devon continued to build his business, using his Uncle Ralph as a consultant and mentor to the two new employees he hired. He got together with his siblings and their families whenever possible and even made time to see his friends Pat and Eric. Devon, Pat, and Eric fished and hiked together in their favorite hardwood forest, wearing their old worn *Butter Capital of the World* hooded sweatshirts.

Vern called around the end of that breakout year. He casually mentioned to Devon that Yvonne had moved back to the area; she had a job at the Mohonk Mountain House in the events planning department. Before hanging up, Vern added, that Yvonne had been divorced for five years and had two daughters.

Devon sat near the phone, flooded with memories of Yvonne. He hadn't been to Mohonk all year, and it was only a short drive from his cabin. When Devon went to reach for his car keys, the **Presence Key** caught his eye. Devon was free!

The Devon Sims Story and Prison Break Model

Prisoner by:

Negative self-Talk

> I should

Goal Setting (The Setup)

> No. 2. You try to meet a goal someone else set for you.

> No. 3. You set a goal that is unrealistic to accomplish, for the person you are, at the time of setting. Of course these are not unrealistic goals if you are Mother Theresa, the Bionic Man, or Hercules.

Unhealthy Relationship Choices

> No. 5. You choose someone who is <u>so</u> different from you.

Forts/Prisons:

> Fear of the Unknown
>
> Too Nice
>
> Guilt
>
> Worry
>
> Avoidance of Pain
>
> Unhealthy Patterns

Jailers:

> Hugo First
>
> I.E.Magine
>
> Jason Wall

Prison Break Keys:

> NJSO
>
> Self-Questioning
>
> Courage
>
> Healthy-Risk

> Patience
>
> Self-Trust
>
> Presence
>
> Self-Acceptance

Prison Break Story No. 5: Earl Alvarez

The story of Earl Alvarez is our last Prison Break story. You briefly met Earl in Chapter Two, on Unhealthy Relationship Choices. Earl had a very bumpy road from his young life as a Fort Builder to the numerous attempts at Prison Breaks in his adulthood.

Earl was born in Baja, California. His family of eight moved to Miami when Earl was four years old. His father, John, had made a living bartending in Baja. A friend told him there was an opening for a bartender on Carnival Cruise Lines, based in Miami. The job offered a good benefits package and potential for a much higher salary. Earl's grandparents and his uncle lived together in Miami and said that they would help out with the children when John was away on the cruises. This offer was the deciding factor.

Earl's family couldn't afford a house when they first moved to Miami, so they rented a three-bedroom, two-bathroom apartment in North Miami. Rosa, Earl's mother, wasn't used to apartment living and was constantly screaming at the children not to be so loud. Three neighbors complained the second week they were there.

Earl's Uncle Luis helped out by watching Earl every Saturday when his father was away. Luis had been in recovery for four years from his alcohol addiction, and the family assured Rosa and John that Luis was sober and could watch Earl. John's parents also watched Frankie, the two-year- old, on Saturdays. The older children were able to play on their own and were watched over by Cara, the thirteen-year-old. While Luis watched Earl, Rosa could get all her errands done without having to put the two youngest children in and out of car seats. She could even find some time for herself. This arrangement was great for Rosa, who was overwhelmed by raising six children practically on her own each time John went out on a cruise.

This arrangement was not good for Earl, because Uncle Luis physically abused him. He was a sick man, and used Earl as a scapegoat for his anger and frustration at not being happy, not being successful, not being popular—all the things his personality made impossible to achieve. Luis hit Earl, twisted his arm, and pushed him around. Earl never knew when his uncle would harm him; there was no rhyme or reason. He was terrorized and believed, in his child's mind, that he was always doing something wrong. Otherwise, why would his uncle keep hurting him?

It was at the early age of four that Earl's forts were created. They were his only means of survival. His constant self-talk (that he wasn't okay, that he must be bad for his uncle to hurt him) made little Earl a prisoner of the **Negative Self-Talk—"I'm Not Enough."** At this same time, Earl laid the groundwork for the construction of the **Prison of Control** and the **Prison of Rigidity**, as a way of bringing order to his frightening and chaotic world. He lived in a world in which he had no voice and no one to protect him. He tried to tell his mother, but since there were no broken bones, only bruises "every child would get," she denied to herself that anything was wrong. She desperately needed her brother-in-law's help.

Earl felt like a victim long before he ever heard the word. At an early age he started to take on a victim persona. He wore it in his expression, wove it into his speech, and projected it in his movements. Earl had gotten pudgy, building a protective wall of fat around him. Also, he found some solace eating junk food. This early **Prison of Victimhood** didn't keep him safe. In fact it attracted, like bees to honey, those who needed to victimize. He was bullied on a daily basis. Earl concluded, from the way he was treated, that something was really wrong with him. He told himself, "I'm a bad person." Earl was ashamed of himself. This shame was the beginning of his incarceration in the **Prison of Shame**, an incarceration that lasted a long time.

The abuse by his uncle continued over the next three years. During those years, Earl was having nightmares. The kids in school who fed on frightened victims were bullying him and he was constantly sick.

Rosa could no longer ignore what she knew deep down. Earl had told her the truth about Luis harming him. Earl's father was puzzled over Earl's night terrors and his constant sickness. One night, when the screams became unbearable, Rosa told John that she thought Luis was hurting Earl. When she admitted that Earl had told her this three years ago, John went ballistic. He made a terrified Earl tell him the truth, and then stormed off to confront his family. Earl knew that he was the cause of the trouble. John cut off ties with his family when he discovered that they had hidden Luis's relapse, and they were once again enabling Luis, this time at the expense of John's son.

When Earl was told that he wouldn't see his grandparents or Luis again, he was sure that he was to blame. The **Prison of Unhealthy Self-Judgment** was added to his growing Prison system. Earl was suffering the loss of another pair of grandparents. The first had been the loss of Rosa's parents, whom he hadn't seen since the family left Baja. Grandparents, a support system that Earl was in desperate need of, were taken away. Earl had a glimmer of realization that his father had protected him, but the anger between his parents that now filled the house made this glimmer hard to hold onto.

The problems between John and Rosa only escalated, with Rosa being under the added pressure of losing the only help she had.

One day, she told John that she was leaving, that she was going back to Baja where her parents would help with the children. She was only taking the three youngest children with her. She said the two older girls, children of John's first marriage, and Earl, should stay with John. She couldn't say the real reason she was leaving Earl behind; every time she looked at him, her shame at not having protected him was unbearable. Instead, Rosa said she felt Earl needed his father. Earl, already feeling he was the cause of his parents' arguments, was now sure he was to blame. He was sure he was so bad that even his mother didn't love or want him.

The **Prisons of Guilt** and **Worry** that Earl had started to build years ago was not enough protection from the painful feelings of abandonment by his mother. This caused him to seek refuge from his intense pain by hiding within the walls of another huge prison complex, the **Prison of Avoidance of Pain**. At this time **Peter Fog**, highly skilled in self-sabotage, cutting criticism, and negative self-talk, became Earl's unconscious, vigilant Jailer. He faithfully kept his post for many years.

John left his job on the cruise line and got a job as a bartender in a restaurant close to the apartment. John got home at 1:00 am and slept until 10:00 am each day, with the exception of Mondays and Wednesdays, his two days off. The girls, now seventeen and thirteen, got themselves and eight-year-old Earl ready for school every morning. Earl often went to school a bit disheveled, which only added fuel to the bullies' fire. He had no friends. When Earl was twelve, he started to hang out with the only kids who would befriend him, the "burnouts."

Earl remained part of this group for the next four years. He was in and out of trouble the whole time. He would steal bottles of alcohol from the local liquor store, and he and his friends would drink in an empty lot behind the school. He cut classes frequently, and his father was often called to school. In his senior year, Earl was kicked out of school when he was caught, for the third time, drinking in class.

When Earl was eighteen and no longer a minor, he was arrested for vandalism. Earl, not unlike his uncle Luis, was an angry drunk. Actually, Earl was angry most of the time, but only when he was high did he act out his buried rage. His long time **Prison of Anger** was to be the cause of his breaking the front window of a store and taking merchandise while intoxicated. He was sentenced to six months in jail. Earl's family was tired of his drunken behavior. Some of the family thought that six months in jail could be just what Earl needed to straighten him out. Others were fearful that jail would only make him angrier and that he wouldn't be able to protect himself from other prisoners. John listened to everybody's opinion, but after two hours of heated discussion, he told them that he had to try to do whatever he could to keep his son out of jail. Through a friend at work, John learned about a program called Drug Court. This program was only available to first-time offenders. The offenders had to work for an entire year and to go to AA meetings every day. If they didn't comply, they were immediately sent to jail to serve out their sentence. Earl's first life break came when he was accepted into this program.

Earl got a job at the library, reshelving books and filling in at the check-out desk. He actually liked this job and the unfamiliar quiet of the environment. He made his first real friends at the AA meetings, he felt they liked him and that he finally belonged to a group. He continued to work at the library and go to three meetings a week after he had met the Drug Court's requirements. He was able to stay out of jail. This was the turning point in Earl's life.

Earl was now twenty-two years old. He was about to make **Unhealthy Relationship Choice #2 You choose friends or a romantic partner whom your "wounded child" recognizes as a kindred spirit.** (This part of Earl's story might sound familiar). One Sunday, Earl was at a garage sale in his apartment complex. He was having a hard time getting the attention of the seller of a trunk he really liked. Suddenly, a lovely young woman asked Earl, "How old do you think that trunk is?" Earl was flustered that such an attractive woman asked him a question, yet he was surprised at how comfortable he felt with her in his space. Earl didn't like people to stand close to him.

After the garage sale, Earl and Bess, the young woman who had asked Earl the question about the trunk, walked to town and had lunch. They talked about their jobs, and how they'd wound up living in Miami. They touched on family, but skimmed the surface, not looking directly at each other during this part of their "getting to know you" conversation. Bess and Earl didn't want lunch to end. Both were thinking that they had never felt so comfortable and safe with someone.

Earl called Bess the next day and asked her on a breakfast date that turned into a sixteen-hour marathon. When Bess mentioned at breakfast that she noticed Earl had a hard time getting the attention of the seller of the trunk, it opened up a floodgate of old feelings in Earl. This was the first time someone noticed how he felt. They took a long walk on the beach and discovered they both had had traumatic childhoods.

Bess had been verbally abused to the point of feeling she had no right to exist. Both of her parents had died and she was taken care of by an elderly maternal aunt. Her aunt took out her unresolved jealousy and hatred toward her dead sister on her niece, who was the spitting image of her beautiful mother. All of her life, Bess felt ugly, useless, undeserving, ungrateful, and all the other "uns" her aunt could throw at her. Her life remained very small and secluded because she used invisibility as a shield to protect her from the rejection she believed she would face.

Earl told her of the abuse by his uncle. He told her about the severing of ties with his father's family, about the abandonment by his mother when he was eight, and a life of being bullied and rejected by his peers. He was afraid to tell Bess about his alcohol and about his arrest. But her quiet and compassionate face gave him the courage to take a risk and tell all. Earl finally had two keys on his small chain, the **Courage Key** and the **Healthy-Risk Key**.

After several months of dating, Bess and Earl continued to share their childhood stories and still took comfort in being heard and understood. After six more months of going over their numerous painful childhood wounds, they realized that they had isolated themselves from everyone else. Isolation was familiar, while trying to expand their world had been difficult for each of them. This developing pattern, of just the two of them, was much safer.

Into their fifth month of seeing each other, Bess decided not to take a trip to London with her aunt— a trip that had been planned before she met Earl but had been delayed several times due to her aunt's ill health. She had cancelled it because Earl looked so upset when she told him she was going. He looked as though he was losing his best friend. His Victim Persona was triggered. Earl's abandonment fears, also triggered, were always right on the surface. Earl wanted Bess with him, especially when he needed to go anywhere that might be crowded and where people could stand too close to him. Bess was a buffer.

Bess and Toby, her only friend at work, had signed up for a self-help course on *How To Be Assertive*. Earl, wanting to protect

Bess, discouraged her from taking the course, saying, "People could be angry if you speak up assertively, and they could say hurtful things if you disagree with them." This only reaffirmed Bess's own fears and she withdrew from the course. Slowly she withdrew from a healthier and more expansive life. That budding voice of health inside of Bess was getting weaker and weaker.

When Bess and Earl married three years later, their silent vow was to protect, over and over and over again, each other's wounded child by constantly reminding each other how unsafe the world was. Four months into her marriage Bess looked out her kitchen window, wondering why she felt so unhappy. Three years later, with the support of her friend Toby and after reading many empowerment books and taking several self-help courses, Bess asked for a divorce.

This propelled Earl into a five-year relapse. During one of his many drunken rages, he seriously assaulted a man at a bar. Earl was arrested and was found guilty. He was given a three-year prison sentence. In hindsight, Earl would realize that this was the best thing that could have happened to him. This was the moment he started to acquire, and put on his keychain, all the Keys he'd need for his internal prison break. This time there would no recidivism.

During his incarceration, Earl was able to have the benefit of a relatively quiet cell and a job in the prison library. He did a lot of self-observation using the **NJSO Key** and let the observation lead to honest **Self-Questioning(Key)**. He asked himself the question, "What do I want?" The GED that he took and passed—an offering by an educational program associated with the prison— and the new enjoyment he had from reading and from learning let him touch the *Self-Trust Key* and the *Self-Esteem Key*. Earl was beginning to know that he was worthy of asking that question, "What do *I* want?"

Earl, in expanding his educational world, had taken posses-sion of another Prison-Breaking key, the *Optimize-Options Key*. By the end of the second year of his sentence, Earl had a thought he'd never had before, "Perhaps I'm not a totally bad person." The *Self-Trust Key* and the *Self-Esteem Key* were again beckoning. These valuable Keys weren't yet firmly in Earl's grasp. At least he was aware that these Keys were available when he had the courage to hold them.

Earl went to AA meetings, another service provided by the prison. He again formed friendships. Lately, when he went to his AA meetings, a strange thing happened to him. Each time he said the words, "I turn myself over to a "higher power," he felt something was missing. The words had a hollow ring when he said them. Earl real-ized that he hadn't yet handed over his shame to a "higher power."

One Key Earl wasn't sure he would ever get hold of was the *Self-Forgiveness Key*. Over his three years in prison, he had learned to forgive his mother, and even to understand why she had left him. She wrote to Earl on a regular basis and had been to visit him four times since his incarceration. But forgive himself?

The day Earl was released, his whole family came to meet him at the gate. When they got home he told them he had somewhere he had to go and that he would be home in time for the big dinner. His family went home to prepare his welcome meal. Earl walked five blocks to the neighborhood church. This was where he intuitively knew he needed to go. A voice deep within him told him this is where he had to go, because the words "higher power" were not enough for the salvation he was seeking. Earl had only recently heard this inner voice. All his life it had been too noisy, too unsafe, and too chaotic for him to hear its call.

Earl was sitting in a pew, head bowed, taking in the silence of grace. He had the *Gratefulness Key* aglow on his chain. When he looked up, a minister was standing at the pew. He asked, in a kind voice, "In what way can I help you?" Earl was free!

The Earl Alvarez Story and Prison Break Model

Prisoner by:

Negative self-Talk

> I'm not good enough

Unhealthy Relationship Choices

> *No. 2.* You choose friends or a romantic partner whom your "wounded child" recognizes as a kindred spirit.

Forts/Prisons:

Rigidity	Guilt and Worry
Unhealthy self-Judgment	Avoidance of Pain
Control	Victimhood
Shame	
Anger	

Jailers:

> Peter Fog

Prison Break Keys:

NJSO	Optimize-Options
Self-Questioning	Self-Acceptance
Healthy-Risk	Gratefulness
Courage	Self-Trust
Self-Forgiveness	

Your Personal Prison Break Model

In each section below, forward your answers (checks) from the (pages) noted on this form: Your Personal Prison Break Model. When you've completed the form, you will know how you make yourself a Prisoner, which Prisons you build, which Jailers you are. Most importantly you will know which Keys you have available to you for your own Prison Break and to become, Your Own Worst Enemy...No More!

Prisoner Role-Negative Self-Talk (Page 9)

I'm not enough   ____

I'm never going to be   ____

I should-be, do, have   ____

Prisoner-Unhealthy Relationship Choices (Page 35)

1. Someone who has the negative traits of the parent you want or wanted to fix/change.

          ____

2. Someone your wounded child recognizes as a kindred spirit

          ____

3. Someone who takes up so much of your time that you can't be present for your own health and development.

          ____

4. Someone who reinforces your negative self-talk   ____

5. Someone who is *so* different from you.   ____

Prisoner-Goal Setting (The Setup) (page 54)

1. You don't set a goal. _____

2. You try to meet a goal someone else set for you. _____

3. You set a goal with unrealistic expectations for who you are at the time of setting. _____

4. You set goals and don't focus on the process. You only focus on the outcome. You give yourself no credit for embarking on the journey. _____

5. You don't examine your nature and personal rhythm. Are you genuinely more of a "be"-er or more of a doer? Is your rhythm more like a Sunday morning or more like a full- throttle Monday? _____

Prison Builder (Page 75)

Prison of Rigidity _____
Prison of Too Nice _____
Prison of Guilt _____
Prison of Worry _____
Prison of Unhealthy Self-Judgment _____

Prison Builder (Page 90)

The Prison of Perfection _____

The Prison of Fear of the Unknown _____

The Prison of Control _____

The Prison of Unhealthy Patterns _____

Prison Builder (Page 105)

The Prison of Anger _____

The Prison of Victimhood _____

The Prison of Shame (a very large
prison complex) _____

The Prison of Avoidance of Pain _____

Jailer (page 116)

Peter Fog _____

Maria Cant _____

Kim Patterson _____

Jason Wall _____

I.E. Magine _____

Hugo First _____

Rosa Pinpointa _____

Master Keys (Page 134)

Non-Judging Self-Observer (NJSO) Key _____

Self-Questioning Key _____

Courage Key _____

Healthy-Risk Key _____

PART VI

YOUR OWN PRISON BREAK

CHAPTER THIRTEEN

Personalize Your Prison Break

This section, as is everything in the book, your choice to use or not to use. If you would like to try this Guided Imagery as a support for your Prison Breaks, you can find a quiet place to sit and read and to slowly take in the guided imagery. You can make a recording and then listen to the guided imagery; close your eyes, sit or lie down in a safe and comfortable location, and let your own voice guide you on a path to freedom.

Guided Imagery

Take a deep breath and slowly let it out. Now let your mind wander as far back in time as it can safely bring you, and see or sense yourself as a young child. Now, see that child on the beach. Take a moment to get a feeling for the child you are at this time. What is that young child wearing? Look at your child's face, what do you see? Smell the salt in the air, feel the warmth of the sun and feel a gentle breeze through your hair.

You, the child, are building a sand fort near the ocean's edge. See this big protective fort. It is important to keep the sand fort from being washed away, so you dig a deep moat to keep the danger of a powerful ocean away from your protective structure. Feel the wet sand under your nails as you dig the moat. Now see your child sitting in the middle of the fort, and, for a while, feeling safe. Experience your child's momentary sense of safety; feel the calmness, breathe it in.

If you can, ask the child what danger the fort is protecting her or him from. Maybe the child doesn't have the words to explain what the danger is. Take a moment to listen and to observe the body language.

Now let's move forward in time. An adult who is maybe too old to build sand forts of protection is standing in front of you. Take a minute to see or sense yourself, the adult, looking back at you. You sense something is not right. You get a feeling your adult is in some way not free, trapped in a false self. Can you feel the truth of that as you look at yourself?

Your sand fort has become a prison that you are trapped in. But what prison could that adult in front of you be in? When you read or hear the names of the prisons, let yourself be pulled to the name that resonates inside you. Let your senses guide you to an awareness of your truth. Read each prison name slowly and feel your response in body and mind. Are you in the Prison of Rigidity? Or the Prison of Too Nice? Let yourself safely know what Prisons you've built. Is it the Prison of Guilt? The Prison of Worry? The Prison of Unhealthy Self-Judgment? The Prison of Perfection? The Prison of Fear of the Unknown? The Prison of Control? The Prison of Unhealthy Patterns? The Prison of Anger? The Prison of Victimhood? The Prison of Shame? Or the Prison of Avoidance of Pain? Which prisons have you unconsciously built?

You can't break out of Prison unless you know you're in Prison. Breathe slowly in and out. Let your prison names show themselves to you. Once they are named, you are ready.

Now picture yourself in a prison cell. It's small, it has one narrow cot, one sink and a toilet and a thin scratchy blanket. Outside your cell is the Jailer. A large-ringed keychain is on that Jailer's belt. These are the Keys that can open your cell door. When the Jailer starts to come closer to your cell, you are amazed to see that this

Jailer looks exactly like you: the same hair, the same eyes, the same nose and mouth. How is it possible? Look again. Yes, it *is* you.

Now, picture that as the Jailer walks away, the keychain falls from the belt, with a loud clang, right outside your cell door. See the sixteen golden Keys. They radiate light. See the light.

You reach and slowly pull the keychain closer. Which Key do you need? As you read the engraved names on each key, let each name resonate within you, let your needed Keys call to you. Imagine yourself using the key(s) to unlock your cell doors. Do you need the *NJSO Key*? The *Self-Questioning Key*? The *Courage Key*? The *Healthy-Risk Key*? The *Patience Key*? The *Change-of-Perspective Key*? The *Success-in-Trying Key*? The *Think-Out-of-the Box Key*? The *Optimize-Options Key*? The *Embrace-the-Unknown* Key? The *Self-Acceptance Key*? The *Self-Forgiveness Key*? The *Gratefulness Key*? The *Self-Trust Key*? The *Self-Esteem Key*? Or the *Presence Key*?

You have decided. Now you have the Key (s). You reach out through the bars and twist your wrist so you can fit the Key into the lock. Experience the sense of accomplishment in finding the right Key for you, and in the effort you put into getting that Key into the lock. Stay with that feeling.

Now turn the Key. Hear the clink of the cell door unlocking. Push that heavy door open. Take in the feeling of freedom, the feeling of awareness, and aliveness. Breathe in the fresh, crisp air, as you walk through the Prison gates.

You are free! You are free! You are free!

NOTES

1. Albert Einstein, letter of 1950 as quoted in the New York Times, 29 March 1972, and the New York Post 28 November 1972.

2. William Shakespeare, Complete Works (Classics Club, Walter J. Black Roslyn, New York,1937), pp.76-106.

3. Don Miguel Ruiz, The Four Agreements: A Practical Guide to Personal Freedom (A Toltec Wisdom Book) (San Rafael, CA: Amber-Allen Publishing, 1997), pp. 1-23.

4. John E. Bradshaw, Homecoming: Reclaiming and Championing Your Inner Child, (Bantam, 1990).Webster's New University Unabridged Dictionary Deluxe Second Edition, (New York: Simon and Schuster, 1983), s.v. "guilt."

5. Ken Moses Ph.D., "Workshop: Shattered Dream & Growth," (Resource Networks Inc., Evanston, IL., 1990).

6. Herant Katchadourian, Guilt: The Bite of Conscience (Stanford, CA: University Press, 2009).

7. Richiele3@aol.com> [FOLKLORE-L] Grandma's Cooking Secret arichiver.rootsweb.ancestry.com,1999.

8. Charlotte Gill, Cut the Ends Off the Roast: Examining the Role of the Individual in the Familial Oral Tradition, (University of Boulder, Colorado, 2014), p.21. Undergraduate Honors Theses, paper 102, as found on scholar.colorado.ed

9. Reinhold Niebuhr, "Serenity Prayer" as found in Winnifred Crane Wygal, Plan Your Own Worship Services (New York: The Woman's Press 1940).

10. Random House Dictionary of the English Language, The Unabridged Edition (New York: Random House,1979), s.v. "anger."

11. Aristotle, The Nicomachean Ethics, as quoted in Daniel Goleman, Emotional Intelligence, (Bantam Books, 1995), p. ix.

12. Source unknown, There is no greater pain, than the pain of avoiding pain.

13. Source unknown, Never ask a question you don't want the answer to.

14. Source unknown, Courage is not the absence of fear, but taking action in the presence of fear.

15. William Edward Hickson (1803-1870), credited with popularizing the proverb: 'Tis a lesson you should heed: Try, try, try again. If at first you don't succeed, Try, try again. It was tracked to the writing of Thomas H. Palmer in his 'Teachers Manual' and 'The Children of the New Forest,' by Fredrick Maryat. Information from en.wikipedia.org.

16. Van Buren Benny, "You've Gotta Have Heart" (lyrics), 1958, in film Damn Yankees.

17. Benjamin Franklin, "In this world nothing can be said to be certain, except death and taxes," from a letter to Jean-Baptiste Leroy, 1789, as found on BrainyQuote.com, Favorite authors.

18. Ken Moses Ph.D., "Workshop: Shattered Dreams & Growth" or "Intensive: Shattering of a Core Dream (Resource Networks, Inc., Evanston, IL., 1990).

19. Random House Dictionary of the English Language, The Unabridged Edition (New York: Random House, 1979), s.v. "self-esteem."

20. Ibid., s.v. "self."

21. Alexander Pope, "To err is human, to forgive divine," line 525 from Essay on Criticism, Part II (1711).

BIBLIOGRAPHY

Aristotle. The Nicomachean Ethics, as quoted in Daniel Goleman. *Emotional Intelligence*, Bantam Books, 1995.

Benny Van Buren. "You've Gotta Have Heart" (lyrics), 1958, from film *Damn Yankees*.

Bradshaw, John E. *Homecoming: Reclaiming and Championing Your Inner Child*. Bantam, 1990.

Einstein, Albert. Letter of 1950 as quoted in the *New York Times*, 29 March 1972, and the *New York Post* 28 November 1972

Franklin, Benjamin. From a letter to Jean-Baptiste Leroy, 1789. BrainyQuote.com, Favorite authors.

Katchadourian, Herant. *Guilt: The Bite of Conscience*. Stanford, CA: University Press, 2009.

Moses, Ken, Ph.D. "Workshop: Shattered Dream & Growth. Resource Networks, Inc., Evanston, IL, 1990.

Moses, Ken, Ph.D. "Workshop: Shattered Dreams & Growth" or "Intensive: Shattering of a Core Dream."

Resource Networks, Inc., Evanston, IL, 1990.

Random House Dictionary of the English Language, The Unabridged Edition. New York: Random House, 1979.

Reinhold Niebuhr. "Serenity Prayer" as found in Winnifred Crane Wygal. *Plan Your Own Worship Services*

New York: The Woman's Press 1940.

Ruiz, Don Miguel. *The Four Agreements: A Practical Guide to Personal Freedom* (A Toltec Wisdom). San Rafael, CA: Amber-Allen Publishing, 1997

Shakespeare, William. *Complete Works: Twelfth Night,* Classics Club, Walter J. Black Roslyn, New York, 1937.

Webster's New University Unabridged Dictionary Deluxe Second Edition. New York: Simon and Schuster, 1983.

ACKNOWLEDGMENTS

I wrote *Your Own Worst Enemy...No More*, to fulfill a promise to myself. To write a book that would help as many people as possible become conscious of the ways they imprison themselves and how to recognize the Keys they already have for their freedom. I wanted it to be clear enough and interesting enough to hold the readers' attention. To write it in a style that allowed the information to be easily absorbed.

Writing a clear book is easier said than done. Any clarity in its present form my book has taken, is due in large part to the people who graciously read, edited, and reedited the original manuscript. Many thanks to Tanio McCallum, a thorough, firm and kind editor. Thanks to Johanna Maria Rose, an editor who uses a fine tooth comb to put the final touches on my usage of language. To Judith Gorman who gently guided me through my endnotes dilemma. My initial readers were Sally Borgman, Rita Lieberman, Vivian Yager, and Jim Evers. Their suggestions were insightful, gentle and they greatly improved the book's flow. Lee Bartow did a studio recording of my Guided Imagery and was patient even on the eighth take. He also advised me on the cover design.

My daughter Justine was the voice of reason, and helped me keep things in perspective. Having loving family and friends, both near and far, makes for a more secure and less lonely environment when engaging in such a lone endeavor.

I am grateful to all the people in my personal and professional life who were the inspiration for my book. Thank you.